CONTENTS

UNDERSTANDING THE MOON

The waxing and waning Moon

This is one of the most familiar features of the Moon as viewed from the Earth. What we are seeing is the Moon's monthly orbit around the Earth (aka the synodic revolution), which starts with the New Moon and takes 29 days, 12 hours and 44 minutes. When new, the Moon is positioned exactly between the Earth and the Sun – thus, the illuminated area of its surface is not visible from Earth. This phase is represented on the diagram below by a black circle. As the Moon progresses on its orbit, it reflects a crescent of light that expands until it is seen from Earth as a luminous disc – the Full Moon. In this phase, the Moon is on the opposite side of the Earth to the Sun. From that point on, the illuminated area decreases until the Moon renews its orbit once more.

The waxing Moon

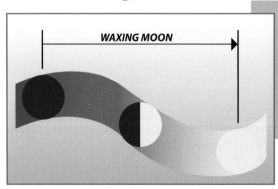

WAXING MOON

The Moon 'waxes' during the phase from New Moon to Full Moon – the illuminated area increases in size every day. On the calendar (pages 56-79), the colour of the blue band also becomes lighter as the Moon waxes.

In the night sky of the northern hemisphere, a quick glance will tell you if the Moon is waxing – the illuminated area is shaped like a crescent, which, if you were to add an imaginary line to the left of it, would resemble the letter 'p'. In the southern hemisphere, the illuminated area is also expanding but is seen the opposite way round, while in equatorial regions the crescent appears to be lying on its back.

This phase is indicated on the lunar calendar (pages 56-79) between the New Moon and the Full Moon.

Plants increase in vitality with moonlight and as the Full Moon approaches, their resistance to parasites and diseases increases. Fruits and vegetables harvested at this time store well and impart more vitality when eaten, while cut flowers last longer in a vase. Silage and mown hay are of better quality, compost is warmer and animals are less anxious when there are people around.

The waning Moon

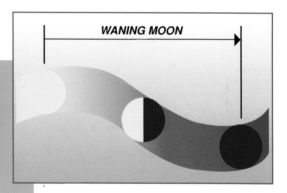

WANING MOON

The Moon 'wanes' during the phase between the Full Moon and the next New Moon. Every night the illuminated area becomes smaller. On the calendar (pages 56-79), the colour of the blue band darkens as the Moon wanes.

In the sky of the northern hemisphere, the illuminated area of the waning Moon reverts to a crescent shape, but now if you were to add an imaginary line to the right of it, it would resemble the letter 'd'.

This phase lasts from the Full Moon to the next New Moon.

As the moonlight decreases, so does the vigour of plants, although their specific energy is increased – colours, scents and tastes are more perceptible during this phase, and nutritional and medicinal properties are more pronounced. However, it is more difficult to store harvested crops in their natural state and this phase is more suitable for preserving foods, making jams and bottling wine. Insecticides and Fungicides are more effective.

The ascending and descending Moon

Many people think that an ascending Moon is the same as a waxing one when in fact they are totally different. The Moon can, for example, wax and descend at the same time. The path of the ascending and descending Moon is similar to the progress of the Sun during the course of the year. In the northern hemisphere, the Sun rises in the south-east and sets in the south-west at the winter solstice, toward the end of December. The arc that it describes in the sky is very short and at noon it is very low on the southern horizon. The closer we are to the summer solstice at the end of June, the nearer to the north-east the Sun rises and the nearer to the north-west it sets. Its arc is much longer at this time and at noon the Sun is very close to its zenith. The sun is therefore ascending during the six months between the winter and summer solstices and descending during the six months between the summer and winter solstices. The Moon also ascends and descends, but over a period of 27 days, 7 hours and 43 minutes, known as the periodic lunar cycle. In the northern hemisphere, the Moon ascends in the sky and then descends again, while in the southern hemisphere the reverse takes place.

On the calendar on pages 56-79, the narrow coloured band beneath the date band shows the path of the ascending and descending Moon in the northern hemisphere as far as the Tropic of Cancer (to determine the path in the southern hemisphere, south of the Tropic of Capricorn, simply invert the colours). Between the two tropics, there is a regular pattern of inversion (see diagram above).

The influences of the ascending and descending Moon and Sun grow steadily weaker the nearer we get to the Equator. Beyond the tropics, the forces that result from such movements are linked with three factors: the ascending/descending Moon, the waxing/waning Moon and the tides (see page 16). Any of these factors can predominate – for example, in Europe, grafting is best done when the Moon is ascending. However, the nearer you are to the Equator, the more the influence of the ascending/descending Moon diminishes, while that of the two other factors increases. For instance, nearer the Equator it is more beneficial to graft plants when the Moon is waxing than when it is ascending.

In the northern and southern hemispheres, in regions beyond the tropics, the ascending/descending Moon has a very strong influence in certain areas of the lunar calendar. In equatorial regions, on the other hand, it is the waxing/waning Moon and the influences of the tide that have greater influence.

The Moon is ascending when, every night, its orbit is higher than the night before. Look at the Moon, ignoring the stars, for two consecutive nights to work out whether it is ascending or descending. On the first night, establish its position in the sky as accurately as possible. A little later on the following night, the Moon will pass through the same vertical once more. If it passes through at a greater height, you will know that it is ascending.

The ascending Moon

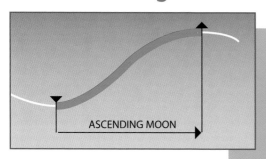

ASCENDING MOON

On the calendar (pages 56-79), the Moon is ascending when it travels from its lowest point (▼) to its highest (▲). This continual oscillation is shown in the illustration. When the curve rises, the Moon is ascending.

The fluids within plants rise and fall with the Moon. When the Moon is ascending, plants contain more sap so there is more activity in their aerial parts (those parts above ground). This is a good time, for example, to cut scions, **to graft plants and to harvest fruit** with a high juice content, as well as to collect sap from silver birches, etc. However, it is better to avoid pruning trees or cutting plants for drying at this time. Cutting lawns when the Moon is ascending tends to encourage plenty of growth; it is a good time to aerate them.

The descending Moon

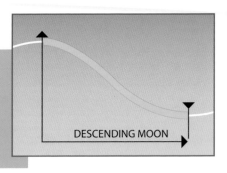

DESCENDING MOON

On the calendar (pages 56-79), the Moon is descending when it travels from its highest point (▲) to its lowest (▼). When the curve falls, the Moon is descending.

When the moon is descending, the flow of fluids in plants descends also and growth occurs mainly in the roots. This is a good time to harvest root crops or the aerial parts of a plant that you want to dry quickly, and also for pruning, pricking out, re-potting, ploughing, spreading compost or manure and cutting wood. The grass of lawns that are cut at this time forms stronger roots and anchors the soil better.

The distance from the Earth to the Moon

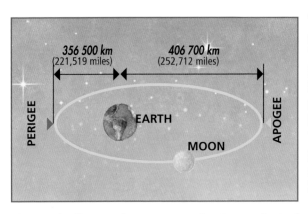

356 500 km
(221,519 miles)

406 700 km
(252,712 miles)

PERIGEE

EARTH

MOON

APOGEE

The Moon moves around an elliptical orbit, with the Earth as one of its foci. This means that the distance between the Earth and Moon is always changing. When the Moon is closest to the Earth, it is at its perigee, and when it is furthest away, it is at its apogee. The progress of the Moon from one perigee to the next is known as the anomalistic lunar cycle and takes 27 days, 13 hours and 18 minutes.

The Moon's effects on plants increases when it nears the Earth and its influence is, therefore, strongest around the time of the perigee. It is advisable to avoid all work involving soil and plants on the day of the perigee itself.

The Moon is closer to the Earth at the perigee; it looks larger at this time and, conversely, smaller at the apogee. In the calendar on pages 56-79, the Moon is shown at its largest near the perigee and at its smallest near the apogee, set in a band that is similarly widest at the perigee and narrowest at the apogee. The point of the perigee is indicated by the letter P and of the apogee by the letter A.

Lunar nodes

The Earth moves in an elliptical orbit, with the Sun as one of its foci. The plane of this ellipse is called the ecliptic. The Moon also moves around an elliptical orbit, with the Earth as a focus. The plane of this ellipse is at an angle of 5° 9′ to the ecliptic. As it moves around the Earth, the Moon therefore crosses the ecliptic twice: once when descending – this is the descending node (☋), and once when ascending – which is the ascending node (☊). Experience has shown that disturbances occur when the Moon is at its perigee or its nodes and these are unfavourable times for cultivating the soil, sowing and harvesting.

On the calendar (pages 56-79), the times to be avoided are indicated in red. Obviously, the closer we are to the nodes and the perigee, the more harmful the influence. Since this influence develops gradually, we cannot indicate precisely when it begins and ends; to get an approximate idea of the hours to avoid, however, simply check the time that the red zone begins and ends.

Planetary nodes

The planets also have nodes, just like the Moon. We have taken them into account up to the present in the last band of the calendar on pages 56-79. This year we include them in the note pages (81–108) using the node symbols (☋ ☊) followed by the appropriate planet symbols (☿ ♀ ♂ ♃).

Eclipses

An eclipse takes place when the Moon is new or full, when it is aligned with the Sun and the Earth in the plane of the ecliptic (2): when the Moon is new it is an eclipse of the Sun and when the Moon is full it is an eclipse of the Moon. When the line of the lunar nodes intersects the Earth's plane of rotation around the Sun and the Moon's plane of rotation around the Earth (1), an eclipse will take place if the node coincides with the New Moon or the Full Moon.

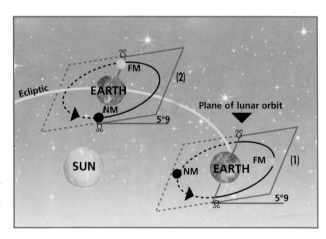

Planes of the EARTH-SUN and MOON-EARTH rotation.

For eclipses in 2012, see the following page.

Eclipses of the Moon in 2012:
- 4 June: partial eclipse reaching its peak at 13:03 (GMT)
- 28 November: penumbral eclipse reaching its peak at 15:33 (GMT)

Eclipses of the Sun in 2012:
- 21 May: annular eclipse peaking at 01:53 (GMT) visible in China, Japan, Pacific and United States (California to New Mexico).
- 13 November: total eclipse peaking at 23:12 visible in northern Australia and the South Pacific.

Zodiac signs and constellations

The constellations of the zodiac are groups of stars, named after their various shapes. These constellations are of different sizes. When the Moon passes in front of, or 'through', a constellation, it activates the influences belonging to it and transmits them to us. We owe our understanding of the laws concerning the Moon in the constellations to Rudolf Steiner, the father of anthroposophy. In 1924, he became the founder of biodynamic cultivation and his work has promoted the development of different systems of organic farming.

Centuries ago, the Chaldeans of Mesopotamia imposed a regular structure on the constellations, dividing them into 12 equal parts of 30° in order to mirror the length of their year. These divisions were called signs and the system will be familiar to followers of sun-sign astrology (dates when the sun changes sign and constellation are included, for information only, on the calendar on pages 56-79). The zodiacal year begins with the sign of Aries in spring, at one of the two points in the year (vernal and autumnal) where the ecliptic

crosses the celestial equator (imagine the plane of the terrestrial equator extending into space). In biodynamics (see page 19), the same regular structure is imposed on the lunar cycle. An astronomical phenomenon means that the natural rhythm of the constellations does not correspond exactly with the 'imposed' rhythm of the signs, and because the influences of constellations and signs are different (see below), both are used in biodynamics, sometimes in harmony (see page 10).

The influence of signs and constellations is not the same: signs affect energy by influencing the fundamental qualities (hot, cold, dry, wet), whilst constellations influence the roots, leaves, flowers and fruits of the plant. Humans and animals are more sensitive to signs, plants to constellations.

The Moon in the zodiac signs

The four fundamental qualities (hot, cold, dry, wet) act upon plants largely through the signs of the zodiac.

Hot tends to assist and accelerate plants' metabolism and helps in the exchange of fluids. Crop production is increased. However, if you actively increase heat, plants could dry out, particularly if there is already internal or external dryness. If there is already too much internal or external moisture, the risk of contracting parasitic or viral diseases increases. 'Hot' helps to counter-balance excessive external 'cold'.

Cold tends to slow down the development of the plant, hinder the exchange of fluids and limit metabolic changes. It also improves resistance to heat.

Dry tends to limit the amount of water in the tissues, concentrates the sap and helps to resist external moisture. Too much can cause the plant to mature too rapidly and wither.

Wet governs the amount of water in plants, which can reach more than 99% of plant mass. It stimulates active principles and nourishes the whole plant. Excess fluid can lead to decomposition and rotting.

- The expansive and vapourizing effects of 'wet' by 'hot' creates AIR. Air is therefore hot and wet.
- The condensation of 'wet' by 'cold' creates WATER. Water is therefore cold and wet.
- The concentration of 'cold' by 'dry' creates EARTH. Earth is therefore cold and dry.

It is not possible, therefore, to apply one quality in isolation. If you want to apply the quality 'dry', you must choose DRY and COLD (in other words, an EARTH sign) or DRY and HOT (a FIRE sign).

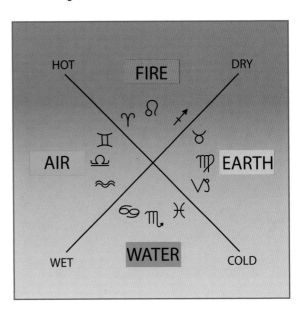

- These qualities cannot exist in isolation; they combine to create the four elements.
- The intensification and concentration of 'hot' by 'dry' creates FIRE. Fire is therefore dry and hot.

For example, if you want a specifically dry effect, work alternately when the Moon is in an Earth sign and when it is in a Fire sign; the alternate hot and cold qualities cancel each other out and the dry effect of your work will remain.

The Moon in the constellations

When the Moon is in a Fire constellation (Aries, Leo, Sagittarius), plant activity is concentrated mainly in the development of fruits and seeds. It is a good time for growing tomatoes, French beans, peas, apples and cereals of all kinds (and for maintenance and planting seeds, where appropriate).

When the Moon is in an Air constellation (Gemini, Libra, Aquarius), the flowering part of a plant grows well, so this is a positive phase for cultivating vegetables such as cauliflowers and artichokes, and ornamental flowers.

When the Moon is in a Water constellation (Cancer, Scorpio, Pisces), the leaf parts of plants grow well. Now is the time to work on salad vegetables, spinach, chard and so on.

When the Moon is in an Earth constellation (Taurus, Virgo, Capricorn), bark and roots develop well, making it an ideal time to concentrate on carrots, potatoes, asparagus, celery, parsnips and other root vegetables.

When signs and constellations are aligned

Better results are achieved when certain signs and constellations are aligned. We have concentrated on the effects of these alignments on food and wine crops, but further observations will allow us to focus and expand on the effects on other plants.

These alignments are represented in the bands on the calendar (pages 56-79) by letters of the alphabet. For example, 'p' indicates that the sign of Leo coincides with the constellation of Cancer. Varying shades of grey indicate periods corresponding to a letter and the times of changes are noted within the signs and constellations bands.

Planetary aspects

The planets revolve around the Sun at different distances and speeds. Viewed from the Earth, they move constantly across the sky. If we look at two planets at any given moment, they form an angle of which the Earth is the apex. If we see these two planets in alignment, the angle formed with the Earth is 0°. When this happens, they are in conjunction. When one planet sets and the other rises, it is known as an opposition (180°). When the position of a planet creates an angle of 60°, 90° or 120°, it is in aspect. Each aspect has been given its own colour in order to make location easier.

- ■ An angle of 0° is a conjunction (♂), represented by ♂
- ■ An angle of 60° is a sextile (✳), represented by ✳
- ■ An angle of 90° is a square (▢), represented by ▢
- ■ An angle of 120° is a trine (△), represented by △
- ■ An angle of 180° is an opposition (☍), represented by ☍

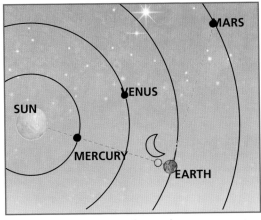

In the illustration, the Moon is in conjunction with Mercury and the Sun (☽ ♂ ☿ ☉) and also square to Mars (☽ ▢ ♂).

Some of these aspects can promote the harmonization of energy, leading to healthier growth. Others can disrupt the plant's energy, causing such problems as slow growth, excessive growth and disease.

In several chapters, we refer to planetary aspects - the days and times of these are indicated in the following pages.

We have observed that some aspects play a major role in various domains, during a time scale varying from a few hours to a whole day. You too can make your own observations and use planetary aspects in other ways than listed here.

For instance, checking in the tables that follow one of the moon's planetary aspects is: January 1 at 06:00 when the Moon is in square to sun (☽ ▢ ☉).

JANUARY

Columns: days 1–31

	☉: SUN	☿: MERCURY	♀: VENUS	♂: MARS	♃: JUPITER	♄: SATURN	♅: URANUS	♆: NEPTUNE	♇: PLUTO

FEBRUARY

Columns: days 1–29

	☉: SUN	☿: MERCURY	♀: VENUS	♂: MARS	♃: JUPITER	♄: SATURN	♅: URANUS	♆: NEPTUNE	♇: PLUTO

MARCH

Columns: days 1–31

	☉: SUN	☿: MERCURY	♀: VENUS	♂: MARS	♃: JUPITER	♄: SATURN	♅: URANUS	♆: NEPTUNE	♇: PLUTO

APRIL

Columns: days 1–30

	☉: SUN	☿: MERCURY	♀: VENUS	♂: MARS	♃: JUPITER	♄: SATURN	♅: URANUS	♆: NEPTUNE	♇: PLUTO

12

Choose a receding tide for these tasks:
- sowing, when the Moon is ascending to balance energies
- pricking out
- cultivating light soil
- cutting wood
- harvesting, when the Moon is waxing

Tidal influences are not felt immediately, and with plants, the delay is estimated at about an hour. For example, the first effects of a rising tide will be felt about one hour after the Moon rises or sets; the effects will continue until one hour after it reaches the meridian. In the time (up to thirty minutes, in fact) that precedes or follows the change, the effect will be greatly reduced, so avoid these times if you want to get the maximum benefit from your work. The effects of a rising tide are stronger in the morning, while those of a receding tide are stronger in the afternoon. This pattern occurs near the New Moon and the Full Moon; tidal influences are weaker around the 'quarters'.

The times given in the notes pages (81–108) are for GMT standard time (26 October to 29 March) and British Summer Time (30 March to 25 October) – see page 80 for other countries.

The times given for the rising and setting of the Moon are for London. For the times for where you live, see the table, page 80.

On pages 81-108, to make the calculations easier, the time that a rising tide begins to affect plants is marked in green and the time that a receding tide begins to affect plants is marked in black. The times for London are valid for a good part of England. For greater precision, see the time differences marked on the map, right.

TIME DIFFERENCES FROM LONDON

+ 40   +30   +20   +10   0   -10

For Ireland add 30 minutes to the times indicated. For example, if you want to carry out a crown graft on 9 May and benefit from the effect of the rising tide, do it between 09:00 and 17:30 if you are in the London area. If you are in Ireland, do it between 09:30 and 18:00.

Chinese seasons

The traditional Chinese year is made up of 12 lunar months (13 months in 7 years out of a 19-year cycle), each month beginning at the New Moon and lasting 29 or 30 days. The Chinese New Year takes place between 21 January and 20 February. Chinese springtime is determined by the Sun and begins halfway between the winter solstice and the vernal (spring) equinox. Between each season comes an 'inter-seasonal' period of 18 days that makes it easier to adapt to the change from one season to the next. According to traditional Chinese culture Qi (pronounced chi) is the energy or 'life force' that is present everywhere in the universe and that flows around us as part of that universe. The seasons influence the nature of the Qi. The five elements (wood, fire, earth, metal, water), and all that is linked to them, form the basis of Chinese culture and medicine (see the table below). The main focus of Chinese medicine is on the prevention of illness by taking into account the rhythm and flow of the Qi – treating the patient at the appropriate time enables treatment to work more effectively.

The method used in acupuncture is simple and effective – treatment is given during the inter-seasonal period before the season that governs the part of the body that is affected. For example, for problems involving the element 'water' (such as bladder, kidneys, fatigue and anxiety), treatment is carried out between autumn and winter. By taking into account the patient's Qi, the most effective days for treatment can be selected. As a result, knowledge of the Chinese seasons is extremely useful for practitioners whose work involves energy flow.

ELEMENT	WOOD	FIRE	EARTH	METAL	WATER
SEASON	Spring	Summer	Inter-season	Autumn	Winter
DIRECTION	East	South	Centre	West	North
ORGAN	Liver	Heart	Spleen	Lung	Kidneys
VISCERA	Gall bladder	Small intestine	Stomach	Large intestine	Bladder
TASTE	Acid	Bitter	Sweet	Pungent	Salty
COLOUR	Greeny blue	Red	Yellow	White	Black
ORGAN/SENSE	Eye/sight	Tongue/speech	Mouth/taste	Nose/smell	Ear/hearing
EMOTIONS	Anger	Joy	Thoughtfulness	Sadness	Intense fear
ENERGY	Wind	Heat	Wet	Dry	Cold

Para Magnetism

The Earth is an electromagnetic body, with its own electromagnetic grid pattern. This grid has an effect on all living things and includes telluric lines, underground streams, ley lines and geological fault lines.

For the past fifty years, physicists, doctors and dowsers have demonstrated how a specific location, or soil, can influence the growth or behaviour of plants, trees, animals and people. Dr Hartmann and Dr Curry are both well-known exponents of the theory, having highlighted the existence of electromagnetic fields.

This sickly tree has suffered as a result of being planted on an intersection of electromagnetic lines (causing the double trunk, canker, stunted appearance, smaller leaves and fruit).

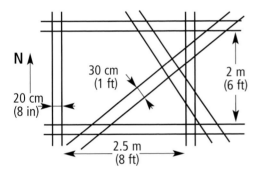

N

30 cm (1 ft)

2 m (6 ft)

20 cm (8 in)

2.5 m (8 ft)

The **Hartmann** Grid consists of naturally occurring charged lines measuring 20 cm (8 in) in width and occurring at intervals of, on average, 2 m (6 ft) running from north to south and 2.5 m (8 ft) from east to west. The grid is like a large-meshed fishing net covering the Earth, and its influence can be felt even at the top of the highest buildings. The **Curry** lines measure 30–40 cm (12–16 in) in width and run diagonally to the Hartmann lines and at irregular intervals.

Many animals avoid the lines, including dogs, cattle, horses, pigs, deer, stags and wild boar. Others are drawn to them, such as cats, ants and swallows.

It is advisable not to spend too much time where the lines occur and to take great care over the positioning of furniture and equipment, including beds, workstations and the chair used regularly for watching television. It is important to remember that every living thing positioned directly above the intersection of these lines (the nodes) will be adversely affected at some stage. Pay particular attention to where you plant trees and shrubs and position beehives and animal hutches.

You may already have experienced the effects of electromagnetic fields. If not, it is relatively easy to locate the fields after a few lessons on using a divining rod, a dowsing pendulum, a Hartmann lobe or your own hands.

Hartmann lobe

WORKING WITH THE MOON

> Each time we cultivate the soil, we can modify or increase any influences. If you have sown a crop at an unfavourable time, you can reverse the effect to a certain degree by hoeing at a favourable time.

SOWING: Our trials showed that seedlings are mainly influenced by the constellations, the planetary aspects and the waxing or waning moon. The role of the Moon ascending or descending is secondary. It may however be useful to take into account for plants that sprout easily such as summer salads. Sowing during the constellation "Leaves" and waning moon will delay seedling growth.

In conclusion: Always choose the constellation that corresponds to the purpose sought (roots, leaves, flowers or fruit) if possible with the maximum number of stars, because they are the combination of both lunar and planetary influences (see the last line curves p.56 to 79). Sow preferably in the morning.

PLANTING AND PRICKING OUT: choose days when the Moon is descending and also, if possible, when it is opposite a constellation appropriate to the crop that you are growing (ie. favourable to fruit, root, flower or leaf plants) and preferably in the afternoon.

HOEING: for eradicating weeds see page 33.

IN WET WEATHER: if possible, weed in the morning in a Fire or Air sign when the Moon is waning.

IN DRY WEATHER: weed in the evening, if possible, and in an Earth or Water sign when the Moon is waxing.

WATERING: to avoid plants developing shallow roots, instead of watering little and often, water them generously but less frequently. The ideal time is when the Moon is in the descendant and in the constellation of Virgo, Gemini or Libra. Avoid nodes and the superposition of the sign of Leo with the constellation of Leo.

MULCHING: mulch helps to fertilize and protect the soil, and limits the evaporation of moisture and weed germination.

A variety of materials can be used as mulch, such as straw, grass cuttings (a thin layer, fresh or dried), composted bark (very effective, a thickness of 2 or 3 cm/about 1 inch is enough).

It is best to mulch when the Moon is waxing and in an Earth or Air sign.

Aeration of the soil should ideally be carried out when the Moon is ascending; soil decomposes and breaks down more easily (via worms and micro-organisms) when the Moon is descending.

STRAWBERRIES: separate and plant out runners during the constellation of Leo ♌ preferably when the sign of Leo ♌ is in superposition with the constellation of Leo ♌ (♌) for example, from July 20 at 21:00 (GMT) to July 21 at 18:25 (GMT).

THE END PRODUCT: always bear in mind the kind of crop you are growing. Take endives as an example – sow and hoe them on dates favourable to 'root' plants in order to help the roots develop well, but, to ensure a good crop, harvest them on dates favourable to 'leaf' plants when the Moon is descending. Their growth should be forced on a good 'leaf' date when the Moon is ascending.

GREEN SALAD: until July, sow green salad in a Water constellation when the Moon is waning in order to prevent these plants from going to seed. During the autumn many forms of energy are in decline. To compensate, sow green salad in a Water constellation, but when the Moon is waxing.

POTATOES: plant potatoes on a day favourable to 'root' plants, but not too close to the perigee. To raise seed potatoes, plant when the Moon is in the sign of Taurus.

To avoid producing green potatoes, earth up when the Moon is in an Earth constellation and when it is waning and also, if possible, with a receding tide.

To remove the eyes (buds) from potatoes that have been lifted and stored so that they will keep longer, choose a time when the Moon is waning and descending, and preferably when it is in the constellation of Virgo.

CROP ROTATION: see page 32.

Seeds

Generally, harvest the seeds in dry weather, when the moon is waxing, avoiding the first and the last day of this phase. Also avoid lunar nodes and times when the Moon is squared with either the Sun or with Saturn.(☾ ◻ ☉ - ☾ ◻ ♄).

• **Fruits:** harvest them on a 'fruit' date and wait for a day before extracting the seeds, for instance: tomatoes harvest on August 10 and extract seeds on 11.

• **Roots:** harvest the seeds on a 'root' date.

• **Flowers:** harvest the seeds when the moon is in the constellations Gemini or Libra.

• **Leaves:** harvest when the moon is in an air or earth sign.

Daily rhythms

The Earth's energy patterns vary according to the seasons. During spring, when the Sun is ascending, the Earth 'breathes out', whereas in the autumn, the Sun descends and the Earth 'breathes in'. The same pattern is echoed by the Moon when it is ascending (sometimes called the lunar spring) and when it is descending (also known as the lunar autumn). And energies rise and fall throughout the day too, rising in the morning when the Earth 'breathes out' – a good time to sow (for example, carrots during the morning of a day favourable to 'root' plants), to weed in wet weather, and to harvest aerial plant parts. In the afternoon, the Earth 'breathes in' so it is a good time to plant, prick out, plough, weed in dry weather and harvest root crops. The intervening period, from 12:00 to 15:00, is a period of transition and is best avoided.

CARROT Apiaceae family

Description : A biennial plant native to Asia and Europe. The first carrots were quite tough and yellow or violet in colour. The orange varieties appeared in Holland 3-4 centuries ago due to genetic selection. The root has a sweet and mild taste and can be eaten either raw or cooked; it can easily be incorporated into most recipes. The feathery tops are rich in vitamins and can be used in soups.

Climate: Carrots are able to adapt to grow in most climates they are resistant to mild frost (about -5 °).

Soil: Carrots grow best in light, stone free, well drained, fertile soil, the roots cannot penetrate or swell in heavy clay or compacted soil. Rich sandy soils and a fine seedbed provide the best conditions for the carrot roots to penetrate deeply and to grow well. Practice a 3 or 4 year rotation cycle when growing carrots .

Fertilizer: Dig in approximately 2 kilos (4.5 pounds) of well-rotted compost or manure the previous autumn. Excess nitrogen and fresh manure will cause root splitting and attract pests and diseases.

Varieties: There are many good quality varieties, classified according to their length. Short carrots are grown for a quick harvest and the long varieties for over wintering. Some examples of the most popular varieties are: Amsterdam, Autumn King, Chantenay, Flyaway, Nantes, Nanduri, St Valerie and Yellowstone.

Sowing: Sow in open ground from March onwards for summer eating. Sow in May and June to grow for over winter storage. Sow in drills about 15cm (7 in) apart. To limit thinning, sow seed thinly to start with. Cover with up to 1cm (.5in) of soil. Germination takes place between 8 days and three weeks depending on the temperature. Thin in stages to about 4-5cm (1.5-2in) apart. When the soil is dug deeply or hoed it is exposed to air and light and this leads to the germination of weed seeds contained in the soil. For soils that do not compact too much, prepare the ground 10 to 15 days before sowing. Then simply rake the surface of the soil at the time of sowing to kill the weeds that have germinated. This technique limits the need for subsequent weeding.

Care/ Maintenance: Check for slugs during the first few weeks. Hoe and weed regularly. Ridge up very slightly to bury the top of the carrot as this helps to prevent the carrot fly. To avoid this, also practice companion planting, for example, leeks, garlic or onions. In fact anything that masks the scent of the carrot will help to prevent the fly. Putting coffee grounds on the seedlings, spraying with a decoction of tansy, lavender or garlic is very effective especially if this is repeated every two to three weeks. It is also possible to cover with this fleece. To avoid the roots splitting during a dry spell, especially if the soil is well-drained, water from time to time. The carrot is not a difficult vegetable to grow and if you follow the directions regarding crop rotation and companion planting, there is little risk of disease.

Kept cool and protected from insect attacks, in March the carrots will be just like they were when they were harvested in October.

Harvest: The carrots approximately 3 months after sowing. Harvest the carrots for over winter storage in October and November, during dry weather when the moon is waning. Lift the carrots and remove most of the foliage allowing them to dry slightly before storing in a clamp or root cellar. An ideal way to store for domestic consumption is to use a washing machine drum (see photo), in well-draining soil. For easy and regular access to the carrots, bury 3 / 4 of the drum and cover with straw or leaves, then a final covering with soil. You can also keep them in the ground if the soil is well-drained and there are no voles. In this case, cover the carrots with a small mound of soil and protect them from the cold using fleece.

CELTUCE or asparagus lettuce
The Asteraceae (Compositae) family

Description : A romaine type, non-hearting lettuce, of mid-Eastern origin, with long, lanceolate or slightly rounded leaves depending on the variety. Celtuce is mainly cultivated for its stems, from 3 to 6cm in diameter that are produced just as the plant bolts. Celtuce is refreshing, crisp and juicy, and retains its beautiful green colour when cooked. It is delicious steamed like asparagus or sauted cut into strips or slices.

The flavour is refined and delicate, faintly recalling butter lettuce and hazelnuts. The young leaves can also be eaten.

Climate: Celetuce prefers a temperate climate.

Soil: Requires a soil rich in humus, lightweight, moist and cool.

Fertilizer: Dig in well-rotted organic matter before planting, the Celtuce stems will be thicker or thinner depending on how well-rotted the compost was.

Sowing: Sow in the open ground or in the trays or modules in the greenhouse (in this case, transplant during the waning moon) on a "leaf" day; sow every 10-15 days from March to July. The best results are obtained with seedlings from April to June. Space the seedlings 20 to 25 cm apart and in rows at least 30cm apart. Grow in an sunny location and mulch after planting to conserve moisture.

Varieties: The most common variety is the "celtuce". There are also the "Pamirasparagus lettuce "and"Crakow" varieties.

Care/ Maintenance: Celtuce does not like excess, nor cold nor hot. It requires regular watering, otherwise it becomes tough and bitter. Hoe regularly or mulch to reduce evaporation. During bolting, bottom leaves can be removed to prevent rot. It is sensitive to the same diseases as ordinary lettuce, mostly mildew and rot if lack of ventilation.

Harvest: Two to two and half months after sowing when the stems reach 40 to 50 cm. Peel them, especially the outer stem which is fibrous. They will keep a week in the bottom of the refrigerator.

Horticulture

BULBS: plant bulbs when the Moon is in the constellation of Libra (♎).

REPOTTING: repot plants when the Moon is descending.
- Choose a date favourable to 'leaf' plants for those grown for their foliage (♋ or ♍).
- For flowering plants, choose a date favourable to 'flower' plants (♊ or ♎).

FERTILIZING: add fertilizer when the Moon is descending and if possible, when it is waxing, avoiding Fire signs.

GRAFTING ROSES: shield budding can be carried out during any month of the year on a date favourable to 'flower' plants when the Moon is ascending. Graft as low down the stem as possible towards the base to prevent suckers from forming.

PRUNING ROSES: choose a 'flower' date when the Moon is descending. All roses should be pruned when they are dormant or semi-dormant, ie. between autumn and when the buds are just beginning to break out in the spring, but avoiding frosty periods. Prune to an outward facing bud, removing dead, diseased and dying shoots and any crossing growth. Pruning will also help to prevent damage to tall stems caused by wind rock. Most modern roses flower on new or the current season's growth and so should normally be pruned fairly hard to stimulate new growth and to encourage flowering. Shrub and old garden roses should be pruned lightly.

- **Cluster-flowering bush roses (Floribunda):** cut back main stems to 30–40 cm (12–16 in) from the ground or, for taller cultivars, to about one third of their length.
- **Large-flowering bush roses (Hybrid Tea):** cut back to 20–25 cm (8–10 in) from the ground, or slightly less severely in very mild areas.
- **Climbing and rambling roses:** climbers should not normally be pruned in their first two years except to remove dead or diseased stems. In subsequent years shorten side shoots and leave main shoots unpruned unless they are too long. Shorten the side shoots of ramblers in the first two years to a vigorous shoot. In subsequent years cut back old or diseased stems to ground level to maintain a good framework and allow air to circulate freely.
- **Shrub and old garden roses:** prune only lightly – these flower on wood that is two or more years old.

PRUNING FLOWERING SHRUBS: remove dead or diseased stems and any suckers at the base of the plant, retaining the strongest stems. Prune above a lateral bud on a date favourable to 'flower' plants with a descending Moon.

- flowering shrubs (old wood): prune as soon as flowering is over (eg. forsythia).
- flowering shrubs (new wood): prune quite hard when the worst of the cold weather is over at the beginning of spring (eg. buddleia).

Cultivating trees and shrubs

PLANTING

The following rules are important for planting a tree:

Location: avoid very windy positions and see Geobiology information (page 19).

Soil: ensure it is well balanced — for instance, if it is too acidic, add lime-rich material such as spent mushroom compost, if the soil is too heavy, dig in some sharp sand.

Time of year: avoid heavy frosts. It is preferable to plant trees in the autumn, provided that the following winter is not likely to be too hard. You can also plant in spring but you will need to water the young tress more regularly during the following summer. Whichever season trees are planted in they need a lot of attention during their first few years before they become established (watering, aerating the soil, adding compost).

Planting: it is essential to avoid the lunar nodes (do not plant for two days after an eclipse) as well as times when the Moon is square to the Sun, Mars or Saturn (☾ ☐ ☉ ♂ ♄) – see pages 12–14.

- **Flowering and fruit-bearing trees and bushes:** plant when the Moon is descending, if possible when it is also waxing and when the tide is receding. If the Moon is waning, choose a time that corresponds with a rising tide.
- **Deciduous trees and shrubs:** mainly as for flowering and fruit-bearing trees above, except for trees that grow quickly and those that tend to 'rush' (poplars, maples), when it is better to plant with the Moon ascending and waning and with a receding tide. This configuration produces softer wood but it will encourage this type of tree to grow more quickly and with fewer knots.
- **Conifers:** plant when the Moon is in the descendant and if possible waning. This helps conifers such as firs to develop deeper roots.

PRUNING

As a general rule, prune when the Moon is descending, although an exception can be made when pruning a young tree since the ascending Moon will encourage new wood to grow more quickly. Avoid lunar nodes, when the Moon is square to the Sun, Mars or Saturn (☾ ☐ ☉ ♂ ♄) – see pages 12–14 – as well as the perigee, the equinox and periods of severe cold.

- **Fruit trees and bushes**: prune when the Moon is descending, and if possible when it is also waning and when there is a rising tide.

- **Flowering shrubs**: prune when the Moon is descending, and if possible when it is also waxing and when there is a receding tide.

- **Conifers, deciduous trees and hedges**: prune when the Moon is descending, if possible when it is waxing and with a rising tide. However, prune cypress trees, pyracanthas and trees and hedges that have reached their desired height when the Moon is waning rather than waxing.

GRAFTING

Choose an ascending Moon, on a date favourable to 'fruit' plants preferably or on a date favourable to 'flower' plants if this is not possible. Remove and heel in the grafts when the Moon is ascending (in December/January in the UK).

- **Crown graft**: this form of graft is preferable to cleft grafting, which often causes canker and fruit scab. Wait until the rootstock begins to flower so that there is plenty of sap rising and graft on a date favourable to 'fruit' plants when the Moon is ascending, for example 9 May.

- **Shield budding**: this should be carried out in August on a 'fruit' day with a rising moon when the sap is rising for the second time, for example 27 August. To ensure plenty of rising sap, water the rootstock during the fortnight before the grafting. Make the 'shield' from the thin bark of the rootstock, with just a little of the wood attached – by leaving a strip of wood, you prevent the grafted bud from falling out.

PROPAGATING WITH CUTTINGS

Ideally, cuttings should be taken just as the Moon is coming to the end of its ascension and should be planted as it begins to descend.

- **Cuttings from bushes**: (such as gooseberries, blackcurrants, etc.) in autumn, on the last day of the ascending Moon, take cuttings of around 10–15 cm (4–6 in) in length from the current year's growth. Gather the cuttings together in bunches of ten or so, and gently hold the stems together with a rubber band, place them in a plastic bag and leave them for a day in the refrigerator. When the Moon begins its descent, plant the cuttings out at an angle of about 45°, leaving a little less than half the cutting above ground. Planting at this angle helps promote their growth. In spring, as soon as the first leaves appear and when the Moon is descending, gently lift the cuttings and place each in a pot full of enriched peat. A few weeks later, when the roots have developed, plant them out or pot them on in soil-based compost. Propagating cuttings in bunches has been seen to increase hormonal activity, resulting in improved growth.

Harvesting

Various factors influence the quality and preservation of fruit and vegetables after harvest. As a general rule, choose an ascending Moon for harvesting plant parts that grow above ground and a descending Moon for parts that grow below ground, but avoid the perigee, lunar nodes and stormy weather. Fruit and vegetables that do not store well will last much longer if you avoid harvesting during Water signs and constellations (Cancer, Scorpio and Pisces). On the harvesting band on the calendar on pages 56–79, look for the days marked with stars – green stars for aerial parts and yellow for roots.

Other factors to take into account:
- Fruit picked when the Moon is ascending will stay juicy for longer and will have more energy-giving properties.
- The ascending Moon will also help plants to develop and ripen.
- The descending Moon promotes the preservation of certain properties in harvested crops.

As there are many different factors that need to be taken into account we have produced a quick-reference summary:

- Harvest fruit that should be allowed to ripen as slowly as possible (strawberries, raspberries, cherries, apricots, peaches, plums, etc.) when the Moon is waxing and descending (if need be, when it is ascending and waning) and if possible on days with one of the following planetary aspects: (☾ ♂ ✳ △ ♀ - ☾ ♂ ☿ - ☾ ♂ ☍ ☌) see pages 12–14.

- For squashes and varieties of pumpkin that do not keep well, choose a waxing (but not ascending) Moon during the following periods: a - b - i - j - k - L - q - r - s - t - z - (see the calendar on pages 56–79) and if possible pick them during one of the following aspects (☾ ♂ ✳ △ ♀ - ☾ △ ☉) see pages 12–14. For example, AUGUST: 18am* - 18pm* - 19*- 20*- 21*- 26pm*- 27 - 28 - SEPTEMBER: 16*- 17**- 18 before 16:00*- 23 - 24. (am = morning, pm = afternoon).

- When harvesting root crops, follow the guidelines on the calendar (pages 56–79) and try to combine the descending with the waning Moon, except in the case of garlic, onions and shallots, when you should choose the waxing Moon.

We believe that the tides also affect the harvest (see page 16). When the Moon is waxing choose a receding tide and when it is waning choose a rising tide. The best time to harvest crops is when these periods occur in the early morning with dew on the ground, as this gives positive and magnetic energy to the harvested crops.

Plants diseases

On the whole, diseases can be avoided or at least contained through a good soil balance and intense biological activity (microbes and roots). It is essential to stimulate and restructure the soil with the help of living matter. For instance, green fertilizer is one of the best way to obtain such a result. Using 'young' compost can also generate good results in the soil, except for vegetables which require a 'mature' compost.

In most cases, this intensification of soil life will give enough energy to the plants to avoid disease. Plant decoctions also act as a preventative against diseases (see next chapter). Some other products also have a healthy effect on the soil and help prevent diseases. Here are some of the ones we have been testing with success against oidium and mildew.

CHARCOAL

Charcoal reinforces the soil and has a purifying and cleansing effect that prevents cryptogenic diseases in a localized area. It is particularly efficient at preventing the dispersion of spores and seeds. It regulates the soil by assisting in the storage of nutrients. Use natural, pulverized, charcoal, mixed with the soil prior to sowing the seeds, 100 to 150 g/m2. Ideally this should happen during an ascending and waning moon.

SOOT

Soot resulting from burning wood also helps to prevent cryptogenic diseases as it protects the living organisms in the soil. However do not apply if you have already used charcoal, or if the soil is very acid! Mix 200 to 300 g of dry (not wet) soot with 10 litres of water, ideally during a waxing moon (a, b, c, d, i, j, k, l periods), avoiding lunar nodes and Moon-Saturn squares (☾ ■ ♄). Do not use metallic containers, as these can taint the mixture, instead use wood or sandstone. Let the mixture steep for several days stirring every evening; spray on the soil, renew monthly.

BIRCARBONATE OF SODA

Bicarbonate of Soda has the ability to stimulate and re-balance chalky soils, resulting in a decrease in diseases.
Spray onto the soil at dew time a few weeks before seeding, using between 20 to 50 g by litre of water. 5 to 10 g per litre can be used directly on plants in the same way as grapefruit seed extract (see below).

GRAPEFRUIT SEED EXTRACT
(available commercially)

Grapefruit seed extract reinforces and purifies plants, acting as a disinfectant and fungicide. Spray on plants at the dates shown in the Fungicide tables, using 35 to 40 drops per litre of water, or even 50 drops to avoid mildew. Renew every 10 to 15 days, and after rain.

Plant-based decoctions

A plant-based decoction used as a liquid fertilizer provides a natural way of feeding plants and preventing certain diseases. Those made from stinging nettle or comfrey are best known, but other plants can be used such as horsetail, camomile, marigold, achillea or dandelion, either individually or in combination.

Whichever plant you choose, the process for **making liquid fertilizer** remains the same. Cut up the fresh plants into small pieces and soak them in water (use 1 kg/2 lb of plants per 10 litres/15 pints of water) and leave it to steep for between one and four weeks – use a wooden or stoneware container, or even plastic if necessary, never use a metal container. Stir the liquid from time to time to help it ferment; then filter out the plant pulp. Use the resulting liquid fertilizer diluted in the proportion of 1:10–20, as appropriate.

Stinging nettles

Very favourable dates are: MARCH: 22 after 15:00 - 28 APRIL: 21 after 08:00 AUGUST: 26 SEPTEMBER: 25 OCTOBER: 19pm - 24 (am = morning, pm = afternoon). Make the most of the receding tide on these dates to improve the result even more. Liquid fertilizer made from plants should prefer-ably be used when the Moon is descending and, if possible, when it is also on the wane.

WHEN TO MAKE A PLANT DECOCTION

- **To protect against fungal disease:** begin making the decoction when the Moon is wax-ing and, if possible, when it is also descending. The Moon in conjunction, sextile and trine with the Sun (☾ ♂ ✳ △ ☉) as well as superposition (q), will improve its effectiveness even more.
  Favourable dates are: MARCH: 3pm - 6 APRIL: 2 - 3 before 15:00 - 26pm - 30 MAY: 1pm - 26 - 27 after 09:00 - 31am JUNE: 19 after 16:00 - 23 after 15:00 - 24 - 29 JULY: 19 - 21 before 18:00 - 24am AUGUST: 17 after 17:00 - 22 SEPTEMBER: 16 OCTOBER: 15 after 13:00. If you also take into account the influence of the rising tide on these dates (see p16), the result will be even better (am = morning, pm = afternoon).
- **To use as a plant feed:** begin making the decoction when the Moon is waxing, and if possible when it is also ascending. The Moon in conjunction, sextile and trine with the Sun (☾ ♂ ✳ △ ☉) will strengthen its influence.

DECOCTION OF STINGING NETTLE

- To use as a fertilizer follow the instructions top left, leave the nettles to steep in water for three weeks and then dilute in the proportion of 1:10 if it is to be spread on the soil, but in at least 1:20 if it is to be sprayed on leaves.
- To prevent fungal diseases, let the mixture steep for a week and then dilute it in the pro-portion of 1:15–20. The fresh plant can also be used – for example, when potting up tomatoes, put a handful of nettles in the planting hole.

Comfrey

DECOCTION OF COMFREY

A decoction made from comfrey helps combat tomato whitefly, but comfrey really comes into its own as a fertilizer. Fresh leaves can be laid on the soil surface, wilted leaves can be dug into the soil, or it can be used in a liquid fertilizer. To make the liquid feed, soak the leaves in water (see top left this page) for two to four weeks and then dilute in the proportion of 1:10 if applying it directly to the soil or 1:20 if spraying it on leaves.

LIQUID FERTILIZER MADE FROM COMPOST

This is made by mixing one part well-rotted compost to ten parts water and leaving it to steep for one to two weeks. It is effective against cryptogenic (fungal) diseases when sprayed on the leaves of a plant and works on two fronts: it reinforces the plant's immune defences as well as destroying certain fungal spores.

Fungicides and insecticides

We recommend the use of natural products, both for the sake of the environment and to produce a better quality of crop. You can also use liquid fertilizers to prevent cryptogenic diseases such as those caused by fungi (see below and page 27).

A decoction of horsetail is very good for controlling fungal disease. Use about 50 g (2 oz) of horsetail per litre of water (1½ pints) and boil it for 20 minutes. Then dilute with water in the proportion of 1:5 and spray on the leaves or directly on the soil, several times between spring and autumn. If you use sulphur or Bordeaux mixture it is also possible to add horsetail decoction, or

liquid fertilizer made from stinging nettles or compost in order to increase the efficiency and reduce the dosage.

Insecticides: a decoction of comfrey can be used to treat tomato whitefly and a decoction of many other plants can be used to produce natural insecticides, such as wormwood, pyrethrum, English ivy, etc. The table below indicates those dates that are the most favourable for applying insecticides and fungicides. The greater the number of stars (★) the more effective will be the application.

▢ favourable for insecticides
■ favourable for fungicides

INSECTICIDES (spread early morning) and FUNGICIDES (spread evenings)																														
	1	2	3	4	5	6	7	8	9	10	11	12	13	14	15	16	17	18	19	20	21	22	23	24	25	26	27	28	29	30	31
JANUARY																															
FEBRUARY																															
MARCH																															
APRIL																															
MAY																															
JUNE																															
JULY																															
AUGUST																															
SEPTEMBER																															
OCTOBER																															
NOVEMBER																															
DECEMBER																															

Compost

Composting is the process by which animal or plant waste decomposes and breaks down into a substance that is both nourishing and easily assimilated by the soil's micro-organisms. A combination of plant waste and animal manure is normally required in order to ensure the constituents of the compost are in the correct proportions.

The composting process can normally be activated by adding stinging nettles (with their seeds heads removed) and comfrey, either as plants or in the form of a liquid. Good compost should be well oxygenated and loosely packed, not compacted. When it is ready to use, it should be light, rich and have a pleasant smell of humus, so it is important to make it at just the right moment. We have summarised all the different factors that will help you to produce good compost in the table below, including certain Moon/Pluto aspects.

COMPOST

	1	2	3	4	5	6	7	8	9	10	11	12	13	14	15	16	17	18	19	20	21	22	23	24	25	26	27	28	29	30	31
JANUARY					★			★															★	★	★	★★★	★		★		
FEBRUARY	★	★		★									★★	★									★★	★					★		
MARCH	★		★	★								★★	★							★				★		★				★	★
APRIL							★										★						★		★			★			
MAY					★★	★							★	★							★			★							
JUNE			★★	★								★								★	★							★★	★	★	
JULY							★★	★									★								★★	★★					
AUGUST	★			★★	★																	★★	★★					★	★	★	★★
SEPTEMBER										★								★							★	★	★★	★★			
OCTOBER							★					★				★★	★★						★	★	★	★★	★★				
NOVEMBER								★											★	★	★	★★	★				★	★			
DECEMBER	★									★							★	★	★	★★	★				★		★			★	
	1	2	3	4	5	6	7	8	9	10	11	12	13	14	15	16	17	18	19	20	21	22	23	24	25	26	27	28	29	30	31

(★) the more stars, the more favourable the day

▇ a good time to add to or turn compost heaps that generate a high internal temperature (the majority of compost heaps)

▢ choose these dates for working on slower acting compost heaps that generate less heat (often preferred by farmers and gardeners who practise biodynamics)

▇ recommended for surface composting with non-rotted manure (broken down by worms);

▌ a vertical line dividing a date box indicates morning (left) or afternoon (right)

▬ a date box divided by a horizontal line indicates it is favourable for a certain type of composting (green for high temperature compost and orange for surface composting)

MANURE: spread manure when the Moon is descending, if possible on days marked orange (see the table above).

Crop rotation

Each plant has its own nutritional needs and different plants draw nourishment from different layers of the soil. As a result, growing the same plant in the same place can lead to an imbalance of soil constituents and even the depletion of some, along with an increase in parasites, weeds and diseases. In most instances, it is a good idea to wait for three to five years before growing the same crop in the same place again. You can reduce this period, or even ignore it entirely, for vegetables such as spinach and lettuce, which have a short growth cycle. On the other hand, extend the period for crops such as strawberries and asparagus where the plant itself remains in the same position for several years before being replaced, with an annual harvest of just its fruit. Tomatoes are an exception, as they can be grown in the same position for several years in succession.

There are three key rules of crop rotation:

THE FIRST RULE involves rotating plants according to whether they are grown for their roots, leaves, flowers or fruits. On a single plot of land, grow 'fruit' plants the first year (nitrogen-fixing), then 'flower' plants, then 'leaf' (nitrogen-hungry), and finish with 'root' plants. So, for example, you could plant squash, courgettes, maize and French beans, followed by cauliflowers, broccoli or green manure (phacelia, lupins, clover) which would not be cut until the flowering stage; then cabbages, spinach, lettuces and leeks, and, finally, potatoes, celery, beetroots, onions and carrots. You could achieve several rotations in the same year – for instance, green manure could precede or follow a crop. In addition to the rotation of the different crops, it is also important to bear in mind which plants grow well together (see page 110).

THE SECOND RULE is not to grow two plants of the same botanical family one after the other. The main botanical families are as follows:

- **Chenopodiaceae**: beetroot, spinach, Swiss chard.
- **Compositae**: artichoke, cardoon, chicory, endive, lettuce, dandelion, black salsify, Jerusalem artichoke.
- **Cruciferae**: all types of cabbage, cress, mustard, turnip, radish.
- **Cucurbitaceae**: cucumber, marrow, courgette, melon, pumpkin.
- **Leguminosae**: broad bean, French bean, lentil, alfalfa, pea, clover.
- **Liliaceae**: garlic, asparagus, chive, shallot, onion, leek.
- **Umbelliferae**: carrot, celery, chervil, parsnip, parsley.
- **Solanaceae**: aubergine, capsicum, pepper, potato, tomato.

THE THIRD RULE concerns the amount of manure a crop needs. It is good practice to follow a crop that requires large amounts of manure with one that requires little or none.

- **Crops requiring large amounts of manure:** aubergine, celery, cabbage, spinach, fennel, maize, leek, pepper, potato, tomato.
- **Crops requiring little:** garlic, chervil, cress, shallot, broad bean, French bean, corn salad (lamb's lettuce), onion, radish, lettuce.

Other crops fall between the two extremes, requiring an average amount.

Agriculture

ERADICATING WEEDS

- Eradication will be most effective during the days following the full moon, or in the middle of the day – with the best results obtained by combining both together.

- Dig over the soil when the Moon is in the constellation of Leo, which favours germination (marked in ■ in the following table). This will encourage the majority of any weed seeds present in the soil to germinate. Then dig over the soil again to remove them.

- It is possible to contain germination by digging over the soil when the moon is in the constellations of Virgo, Libra and Capricorn (marked in yellow ☐ in the following table).

- **Thistles:** remove thistles when the soil is dry to help prevent them from seeding too easily. They are difficult to eradicate, but for the best results, work in the middle of the day on the dates marked in purple ■ or blue ☐ on the chart below. These dates are also the best for dealing with convolvulus.

CULTIVATING THE SOIL: the work of ploughing, planting, pricking out and spreading compost or manure is best carried out when the Moon is descending. If possible, combine the descending Moon with the waxing Moon when working on light, sandy soil, especially when the weather is dry. In the case of heavy clay soil, if possible, combine the descending Moon with the waning Moon, particularly during wet weather.

- **Dock weed:** dig up dock weed on dates marked in purple ■ or orange ☐.

Choose dates marked with stars (★).
If you have no option other than to dig the soil on dates when there are nodes, dig it over again a few days later to help reinstate positive influences.

If only a part of the day is favourable, the time is indicated by a vertical line (the left section for the morning, the right for the afternoon – see above and left for the key to the colours) ☐. On days that are divided horizontally, two favourable aspects are recommended, as indicated by the two colours ☐.

For example, the afternoon of Jan 22 ☐ is favorable for germination. From 9-1pm is good for pulling weeds.

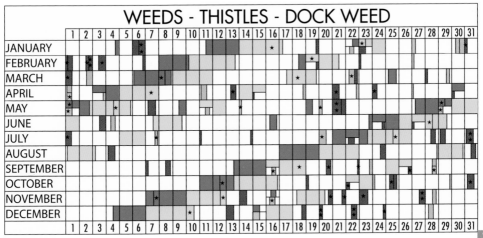

WEEDS - THISTLES - DOCK WEED

CLEARING LAND: to clear land of plants such as thorns and brambles, dig them up or cut them down at the perigee and if possible when the waning Moon is close to becoming new (for instance: DECEMBER : 12, 13am.

MANURE: manure is absorbed by the soil more effectively when the Moon is descending and, if possible, waxing, but avoid spreading manure during Fire signs.

• **Seaweed and natural phosphates** (such as in bone meal): see 'Manure' left.
• **Leaf mould (minerals):** spread leaf compost in the morning (but in the evening if the forecast

is dry and hot), with an ascending and if possible a waning Moon. Avoid Fire signs.

• **Slurry and animal decoctions:** The assimilation, and thus the fertilisation will be better is these products are spread during the descending moon. Taking into account the risk of burning the existing vegetation, it is better to lose a bit of effectiveness and so to spread these during the ascending moon and if possible waxing. In all cases, in water or air signs.
- Lithothamnium calcareum is an acid corrector. Added at 30kg/t, it limits the effects of burning.
- For the same reason, do not spread these slurries during heat waves or frosts.

Hay

• **Quality:** hay will be of better quality if it is cut when the Moon is ascending and if possible also waning. The aspects Moon sextile or trine Sun (☽ ✳ △ ☉) will improve the quality still further.

For example, the following dates will be favourable: MAY: 8 - 9* - 10am** - 10pm - 11* - 12* - 13* - 14 - 16 - 17 - 18am - 18pm* - 19* - 20* - JUNE: 5am - 5pm* - 6 - 7* - 8* - 9* - 10 - 12 - 13 - 14am* - 14pm - 15* - 16* - 18* - 19 before 16:00 - JULY: 4* after 15:00 - 5* - 6* - 7 - 8* - 9 after 14:00 - 10 - 11 - 12* - 13* - 14* - 15*.
(am = morning, pm = afternoon) (in the UK).

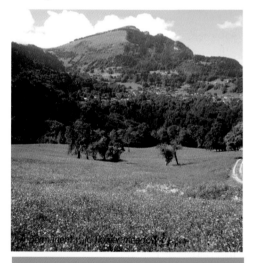
A permanent wild flower meadow.

When cutting hay, always avoid times that are close to lunar nodes, the perigee (including about 6 hours before and after) and the following aspects: Moon square Sun, Mars and Saturn (☽ ☐ ☉ ♂ ♄) (about 4 hours before and 2 hours after).

• **Regrowth:** to promote rapid regrowth, cut hay when the waxing Moon is associated with an ascending Moon.
For example: MAY: 22am* - JULY: 2* - 3*.
(am = morning, pm = afternoon).

Cereal crops

Sow cereal crops on a day favourable to 'fruit' plants, but if this is not possible, choose days favourable to 'flower' and if not 'root' plants. Days favourable to 'leaf' plants are the least beneficial. Also take the following information into consideration to improve results even further. It is organized according to the type of cereal crop.

OATS, WHEAT, BARLEY, RYE

- **Sow:** preferably when the Moon is ascending and if possible waning, with a receding tide.
- **Harvest:** on days favourable to 'root' or 'flower' plants with the Moon waxing and ascending (on dates favourable to 'fruit' plants there is more dust in the air and the risk of weevils is greater, on 'leaf' dates there is a greater risk of fermentation).
  Examples of favourable dates are: JUNE : 5pm - 6 - 7 - 8 - 9 - 15 - 16 - 17am -18 - JULY : 4 - 5 - 6 - 12 - 13 - 14 - 15 - AUGUST : 2 - 3 before 15:00 - 8 - 9 - 10 - 11 - 12am. (am = morning, pm = afternoon). Combine the influence of a rising tide with these dates to obtain even better results. The waxing and descending moon can be helpful with heavy soils.

MILLET

- **Sow:** when the Moon is ascending and if possible waxing.
- **Harvest:** when the Moon is waxing and if possible ascending, but avoid 'leaf' dates.

MAIZE, SUNFLOWERS

- **Sow:** preferably when the Moon is ascending and if possible waning, with a rising tide.
- **Harvest:** when the Moon is ascending, avoiding dates favourable to 'leaf' plants.

OILSEED RAPE

- **Sow:** preferably when the Moon is ascending and if possible also waning.
- **Harvest:** when the Moon is waning and ascending, avoiding 'leaf' dates.

Animal husbandry

COVERING: for cows and mares, the best time is between the first quarter and the Full Moon in Fire and Earth signs and, if possible, with the Moon in the descendent. For ewes, the period between the first quarter and the Full Moon during Earth and Air signs is best, with an ascendant Moon if possible. Avoid the perigee and the lunar nodes if possible.

TRIMMING THE FEET OF LIVESTOCK: carry out this task in the signs of Taurus, Leo, Virgo, Sagittarius or Capricorn when the weather is calm or wet and, if possible, when the Moon is waxing. Avoid stormy or icy periods.

SHOEING: choose the waning Moon, particularly when it is in Earth or Air signs.

WORMING: this should be done two or three days before the New Moon or, if this proves impossible, two or three days before the Full Moon.

CLEANING & DISINFECTING COWSHEDS: this will be most effective when the Moon is waxing and in a Fire or Earth sign.

MATING RABBITS: results will be best between the New Moon and the first quarter.

MALE OR FEMALE CHICKS: eggs collected around the time of the last quarter will produce mainly male chicks. For female chicks, eggs should be collected around the first quarter. For best results, incubate the eggs so that they hatch between the New Moon and the first quarter.

WHEN TO START OUTDOOR GRAZING: choose the following correlations of signs and constellations: a - b - c* - d* - k* - L* - m - n - s* - t* - x (see page 14). For example, MARCH: 1* - 2am* - 2pm - 3 - 4 - 9* - 10pm* - 13 - 14am - 15pm - 16 - 17 before 09:00 - 18am - 18pm* - 19* - 27pm* - 28* - 29* - 30 - 31 - APRIL : 5* - 6am* - 10 -12 - 13 after 09:00 - 14* - 15* - 24pm* - 25* - 26 - 27- MAY: 3* - 4* before 15:00 - 9 - 10 - 11* - 12* - 13am* - 22* - 23am* - 23pm - 24 - 25pm - 30* - 31*.(am = morning, pm = afternoon).

MOVING CATTLE: move cattle between the day after the first quarter and the day before the last quarter, to reduce damage to grass.

BRINGING CATTLE IN: cowsheds will be dryer in winter if cattle are brought inside during autumn when the Moon is passing through the constellation of Leo.

TO AVOID: In addition to the above, avoid turning out, moving or bringing in animals on the following days: JANUARY : 6pm - 9 - 16 - 19pm - 30am - FEBRUARY : 6pm - 7pm - 11pm - 14pm - 19am - 26pm - MARCH : 8 -10am - 24pm - APRIL : 1am - 6pm - 7 - 13 after 09:00 - 24am - 28am - 29am - MAY : 4 after 15:00 - 5pm - 6am - 7 - 25am - JUNE : 3 - 4 - 11am - 17pm - 21pm - 28am - JULY : 1 - 3pm - 4pm - 11am - 25pm - 26am - 28 - 29am - AUGUST : 1pm - 2am - 15am - 23pm - 24 - 28 before 14:00 - SEPTEMBER : 4am - 8pm - 18 - 19am - 20am - 29pm - 30am - OCTOBER : 4am - 8am - 9pm - 17 - 22am - 29 - 31 NOVEMBER : 12 pm - 14 - 20pm - 27pm -28 - DECEMBER : 3pm - 6pm - 11pm - 12pm - 13am - 18pm - 24pm - 28. (am = morning, pm = afternoon).

Beekeeping

BEES

For the best results, work with bees during the following constellations.

During Fire constellations to benefit the queens and increase the production of honey.

During Air constellations to benefit the queens and to encourage the development of young bees.

During Earth constellations to maximise the cell-building instinct. Honey collected during Earth constellations will set more quickly.

Avoid all work with bees during Water constellations – these periods have an adverse effect on the hives and honey.

Extract honey in a Fire or Air constellation.

As a general rule do most of your beekeeping when the Moon is in a Fire or Air constellation and avoid the perigee, lunar nodes and Water constellations.

Winegrowing

PRUNING GRAPE VINES

Prune grape vines when the Moon is both descending and, if possible, waxing, with a rising tide. Avoid the lunar nodes and when the Moon is squared with Saturn (☾ ■ ♄).

DISBUDDING

Disbud when the Moon is waning and, if possible, descending, with a receding tide. Disbudding with the Moon sextile or trine Sun or Mars (☾ ✳ △ ☉ ♂) should reduce the growth of suckers (see pages 12–14).

POLLARDING AND CUTTING BACK

Carry out this work when the Moon is descending, with a receding tide and, if possible, with one of the planetary aspects mentioned above.

HARVESTING GRAPES

An ascending Moon will give a better yield but the wine produced will keep better when the Moon is descending. To improve the quality of the wine and reinforce its character, harvest the grapes according to the constellations. Choose dates favourable to 'fruit' plants for fruity wines, 'root' days for vines grown where the soil plays an important part in the flavour, and 'flower' days for more floral wines. Avoid lunar nodes: they can hinder the development of aromas.

Cider making

DECANT

Decant cider when the Moon is waxing and descending if possible, and with a rising tide. Choose days when the weather is calm, preferably early in the morning with dew on the ground.

BOTTLE

Bottle cider when the Moon is waning and descending, preferably in the constellations of Virgo (♍) or Leo (♌) and, if possible, with a rising tide. Avoid days when the Moon is squared with Mars, Jupiter, Saturn or the Sun (☾ ▫ ♂ ♃ ♄ ☉) – see pages 12–14. Also avoid stormy, windy and very cold weather.

Beer making

WHEN TO START

Make your beer when the Moon is descending and, if possible, waxing, with a rising tide. Moon–Venus aspects (☾ ☍ ♂ △ ✳ ♀), except square, are very favourable. Avoid lunar nodes, the perigee and dates when the Moon is squared with Mars, Jupiter, Saturn or the Sun (☾ ▫ ♂ ♃ ♄ ☉) – see pages 12–14. For the best results use hops picked when the Moon is ascending and with the influence of a rising tide.

BOTTLE

Bottle beer when the Moon is descending and, if possible, between the last and first quarters. Choose a time influenced by a rising tide to help with the development of aromas. Choose an Air sign if possible, and avoid stormy, windy and very cold weather.

Forestry

If possible, only cut down trees after they have lost their leaves, but while the Sun is still in the descendent (before the winter solstice).

TIMBER

Cut timber when the moon is descending but avoiding the first and the last day of this phase. The wood will react differently according to the sign of the zodiac that the Moon is in.

The day on which wood is both cut and used is very important.

- To avoid **parasites** and **rotting**, cut wood in the following signs: Leo ☐, Virgo ☐, Scorpio ☐ or Sagittarius ■.
- To prevent wood from **warping and splintering**, cut it during Libra ☐ or, better still, in Scorpio ☐.
- Cut wood to be used for **frameworks for buildings and other structures** in Leo ☐, Virgo ☐, Libra ☐, Scorpio ☐ or Sagittarius ■.

- Wood for **tools** should be cut in Leo ☐, Virgo ☐ or Libra ☐.
- To prevent the softwood from coniferous trees from **flaking**, cut it in Scorpio ☐ or Sagittarius ■.
- **The superposition of the sign and constellation of Leo (♌) is a good time for cutting wood**, for example from 1pm 4 December to 11:53 on 5 December.
- When the sap is flowing, leave a felled tree for several weeks before removing the branches (the leaves draw out the sap).

Useful tip: to prevent wood from warping when you are using it (for frames, cladding, etc.), choose these dates [☐], especially those marked with stars (★).

In the table below, the signs are represented by colours for easier reference:

Gemini: ■ Cancer: ■ Leo: ☐ Virgo: ☐ Libra: ☐ Scorpio: ☐ Sagittarius: ■

Those planetary aspects that will improve the wood are shown by a star. Those that are harmful are coloured in red ■.

WOOD

	1	2	3	4	5	6	7	8	9	10	11	12	13	14	15	16	17	18	19	20	21	22	23	24	25	26	27	28	29	30	31
JANUARY									★		★★★						★★					★ ★								★	
FEBRUARY					★	★			★	★ ★							★			★ ★					★ ★			
MARCH				★	★	★										★						★ ★			★	
APRIL			★			★	★					★						★ ★				★		★ ★	
MAY	★			★						★					★	★★				★ ★		
JUNE		★									★				★	★★ ★			★		
JULY								★					★	★ ★		★	★	
AUGUST									★		★	★★★★						
SEPTEMBER							★★		★★	★ ★		★					
OCTOBER					★	★ ★★	★	★					
NOVEMBER			★★★ ★	★★ ★			★ ★			
DECEMBER	★		★★	★ ★ ★	★	★ ★	
	1	2	3	4	5	6	7	8	9	10	11	12	13	14	15	16	17	18	19	20	21	22	23	24	25	26	27	28	29	30	31

FIREWOOD: cut firewood when the Moon is descending, avoiding days close to the New Moon. Stack firewood when the Moon is descending, if possible between the first and last quarter – it will dry better then.

CHRISTMAS TREES: cut Christmas trees when the Moon is ascending and waxing to stop them shedding their needles too quickly. The following aspects will strengthen this effect – Moon sextile, trine or square Sun or Venus (☾ ✳ △ ◻ ☉ ♀) – see pages 12-14.

Miscellaneous

WORKING ON BOATS ON DRY LAND: carry out painting work when the Moon is in the descendant during periods (a, b, c, i, j, k). The following aspects can be beneficial: Moon sextile or trine Sun (☾ ✳ △ ☉) and Moon conjunction Jupiter (☾ ☌ ♃). Avoid the nodes and Moon square Sun (☾ ◻ ☉). Return boats to the water when the Moon is waning, if possible between the last quarter and the New Moon and when the Moon is in an Earth or Air sign.

CHIMNEYS: to improve the 'draw' of a chimney in autumn, light the fire during an ascending Moon, on a day favourable to 'fruit' and, if possible, between the Full Moon and the final quarter. Sweep chimneys when the Moon is in the constellation of Pisces between the New Moon and the first quarter.

MOSS ON TILES, SALT DEPOSITS ON BRICK-WORK, MOULD: remove when the Moon is waxing and ascending, avoiding Water signs and constellations. The nodes, the perigee and the Moon squared with the Sun and Saturn (☾ ◻ ☉ ♄) are all favourable, and a drying wind will help.

DRAIN SOIL: when the Moon is ascending.

PATHS AND COURTYARDS: to work on paths and courtyards, choose (the best are marked *):
MARCH: 6 - APRIL: 3*before 15:00 - 30* MAY: 27* after 09:00- JUNE: 3pm - 23* after 15:00 - 24* before 13:00 JULY: 1am - 21* before 19:00 - 28 AUGUST: 24 SEPTEMBER: 20 OCTOBER: 17pm NOVEMBER : 14am.
(am = morning, pm – afternoon) (in the UK).

TRENCHES: the sides of trenches dug or cleaned out when the Moon is ascending may erode more quickly, especially if the soil is light, but should not fall in completely. Trenches dug when the Moon is descending tend to erode and collapse. Choose a time close to the Full Moon to help trenches last longer.

SPRINGS: begin work to collect spring water on the day of the New Moon and when the Moon is ascending (water is lost when it is descending).

MUSHROOMS: usually emerge a few days after the New Moon and are more prolific when the Moon is waxin

SILVER BIRCH SAP: collect silver birch sap when the Moon is ascending, avoiding the nodes and period (f).

PRESERVE FOOD: when the Moon is waning.

SAUERKRAUT: pick cabbages and make sauer-kraut when the Moon is ascending, avoiding the same periods as for bread.

JAMS: jams with a low sugar content will keep better if made when the Moon is waning.

SOURDOUGH BREAD: this will rise well and be extra delicious when the Moon is ascending. If the Moon is descending when baking, ensure that it is also waxing. Avoid nodes, the perigee, the periods (f, o, w), Water signs and constellations, if possible, and the Moon squared with the Sun and Saturn (☾ ■ ☉ ♄) – see pages 12-14.

CLEANING AND MAINTENANCE WORK: will be more effective when the Moon is waxing.

CLOTHES: put clothes away for storage when the Moon is in conjunction with Venus (☾ ☌ ♀) – see pages 12-14.

WOODEN POSTS: to make them last longer, cut them when the Moon is new (or just before) and insert them in the ground when the Moon is in the constellation of Leo. If they are made of softwood, you can also burn the point a little to make it harder.

LAWNS: sow lawns when the Moon is waning and descending on a day favourable to 'leaf' plants or, if necessary, a 'root' date. Aerate lawns when the Moon is ascending on a 'flower' date. To help slow down growth, cut lawns when the Moon is in the constellation of Gemini and Libra or, if necessary, in Virgo or Aquarius. To promote growth, cut lawns in Pisces or, if necessary, in Cancer or Scorpio.

LIVING WITH THE MOON

Do not use the information contained in this chapter as a substitute for medical advice. If you think you have a medical problem, consult your doctor.

Influence of the phases

NEW MOON

• The renewal of physical energy is at a minimum during this phase.
• This is a good time to start eliminating toxins or to tackle a bad habit.

WAXING MOON

• We express ourselves more easily and freely.
• The body makes the most effective use of the nutrients that it receives during this phase.
• If you tend to put on weight, this is a time to be particularly frugal..
• This is an ideal time to learn new skills or to start new projects.

FULL MOON

• Our physical energy levels are restored during this phase.

• When the nights are lighter sleep can be interrupted, and insomnia can be an issue.
• The extra energy and excitement caused by the Full Moon can be channelled into physical activities.
• Now is a good time to undertake a project.
• Some of the effects of the Full Moon and the New Moon can be felt for two or three days.

WANING MOON

• This is a good time for introspection, reflection and spirituality.
• Choose this phase to follow a detox programme; it promotes the elimination of toxins from the body.

Harvesting plants

Waxing Moon: plants harvested during the Full Moon period will have more vitality, but their medicinal properties are weaker than when the Moon is waning.

Waning Moon: plants tend to become dry but their fragrance heightens as the New Moon approaches. Plants picked during this phase will retain more of their medicinal properties.

FOR MAKING INFUSIONS

In the morning while the Moon is ascending: before midday, the Sun's influence is felt mainly on the aerial parts of a plant. It is the ideal time for harvesting leaves, flowers, fruits and seeds, and the effects are enhanced when the Moon is ascending.

In the evening while the Moon is descending: after 15:00 the Sun's influence stimulates activity in the lower parts of plants. This is the time to harvest roots. The effect is enhanced when the Moon is descending.

The following days are harmful: avoid harvesting plants when the Moon is passing through the lunar nodes when ascending or descending or when it is at its perigee (see red zones).

Colt's foot

MEDICINAL PLANTS

Harvesting flower heads (borage, St John's Wort, meadowsweet, etc.): when the Moon is waning and, if possible, also ascending, in an Air or Earth sign. Early morning is best. The following aspects are favourable: Moon conjunction, sextile or trine Sun, Venus and Mercury (☾ ☌ ✳ △ ☉ ♀ ☿) – see pages 12-14.

Borage

Harvesting roots (gentian, marsh mallow, dandelions, etc.): when the Moon is descending and, if possible, also waxing, in an Air or Earth sign. Late afternoon is best. The following aspects are favourable: Moon conjunction, sextile or trine Sun, Venus and Mercury (☾ ☌ ✳ △ ☉ ♀ ☿) – see pages 12-14.

Harvesting from trees (hawthorn, pine nuts, elderberries, etc.): when the Moon is ascending and, if possible, waxing, with the influence of a rising tide and in an Air or Earth sign. The following aspects are favourable: Moon conjunction, sextile or trine Sun, Venus and Mercury (☾ ☌ ✳ △ ☉ ♀ ☿) – see pages 12-14.

Lime blossom

Hairdressing

The table below summarizes for quick reference the best dates and times of day on which to cut hair.

█ a good day for cutting hair to **slow down hair loss**

▢ a good day for cutting hair to make it **thicker and stronger**

(★) **the number of stars** indicates the strength of influence

▓ **not advisable** in any circumstances. Also, to a lesser extent, it is not recommended on days marked with the sign (–)

▌▐ a vertical line indicates the importance of a particular part of the day. The example shows a morning favourable for reducing hair loss and a neutral afternoon

▨ days divided horizontally are favourable for the influences represented by the two colours

HAIR

	1	2	3	4	5	6	7	8	9	10	11	12	13	14	15	16	17	18	19	20	21	22	23	24	25	26	27	28	29	30	31
JANUARY											★ ★		★	★	★				★	★	★		–		–	–					
FEBRUARY			–				★	★	★	★	★			★	–	★	★				–	–	–								
MARCH					★	★ ★	★ ★	★			★		★						–	–	–			★							
APRIL	★	★	★ ★	★	★	★			★	★						–	–	–	–									–	★ ★	★ ★	
MAY	★	★				★ ★	★						–	–								★	★ ★	★ ★	★	★					
JUNE				–	★										–	–	–			★ ★	★ ★	★ ★	★	★	★						
JULY		★							–						–	–	–	★ ★	★ ★	★	★		–							–	
AUGUST																–	–	–	★					★							
SEPTEMBER										★	★ ★	★	★	★	–	–					★										
OCTOBER									★	★	★ ★	★	–	–	–		★														
NOVEMBER				★ ★	★ ★	★	★	★	★	–	–	–	★								–										
DECEMBER		★	★	★	★	★	–			–	–	–																		★	★
	1	2	3	4	5	6	7	8	9	10	11	12	13	14	15	16	17	18	19	20	21	22	23	24	25	26	27	28	29	30	31

The dates marked in this table (█, ▢), especially the starred ones, are highly favourable for hair. Take note of them, even if you have no particular hair problems.

- For more **manageable hair**, choose dates marked in green when the Moon is waxing.
- For a **perm**, choose the superpositions of sign and constellation ♉ ♉ (j) or ♍ ♍ (s) (see calendar pages 56-79), if possible with a waning Moon. It sets better when the Moon is waxing but the hair suffers more damage.
- Hair **coloured** when the Moon is ascending and waxing will achieve better results.
- To help hair **grow quickly**, cut it when the Moon is ascending and waxing.
- If you tend to have **split ends** and/or you want your hair to grow less quickly, we recommend that you have it cut on the following days:

am = morning   pm = afternoon

JANUARY : 9 after 08:00 - 10 after 09:00 - 11 - 12 - 13 - 14 - 15 - 17am - 17pm* - 18 before 15:00 - 19am - FEBRUARY : 8 - 9 - 10 - 11pm* - 12 before 16:00 - 13 - 14 before 13:00 - 15am - 15pm* before 16:00 - MARCH : 8 after 10:00 - 9 - 10 - 11 after 08:00 - 12 - 14 before 14:00 APRIL : 8am - 9* before 09:00 - 10 after 07:00 - MAY : 7 after 15:00 - JULY : 16 - 17am - AUGUST : 12pm - 13am - 13pm* - 14 - SEPTEMBER : 9 - 10 - 11am* - 11pm - 12am - 12pm* - 13 - 14 - OCTOBER : 6 - 7am** - 7pm* - 8pm - 9 - 10 - 11 - 12am - 12pm** - 13 - NOVEMBER : 2 after 08:00 - 3 - 4 - 5 - 6am after 08:00 - 6pm* - 7 - 8 - 9 after 09:00 - 10am - 10pm* - 11am - 11pm* - 30 - DECEMBER : 1 - 2* before 10:00 - 2 after 10:00 - 3am - 4 - 5 - 6 after 15:00 - 7am* - 7pm - 8pm - 9 - 10 after 13:00 - 11am - 28pm - 29 - 30 - 31.

Depilation

The removal of unwanted hair is best performed when the Moon is descending; if combined with the waning Moon, regrowth will be slower. Slow down regrowth even more by choosing certain planetary aspects.

A summary indicating the best dates is shown in the table below. The dates are divided into four categories:

☐ fairly good days   ☐ good days   ■ very good days   ★ excellent days

▌ a vertical line indicates a particular part of the day

DEPILATION

Skincare

SKIN CLEANSING

(Blackheads, impurities, etc.) Treatment works best if carried out when the Moon is in the descendent and in an aspect with Venus (♂, ✳, ▣, △) – see pages 12-14.

NOURISHING THE SKIN

Moisten the skin with dew before applying any cream for best results. Walking barefoot in the dew is good for your general health.

- **Face packs,** moisturizing and revitalizing treatments: the right time depends on skin type.

- **Dry and combination skins:** treatments will be more effective when applied during a waxing Moon. Avoid the following signs: Aries, Cancer and Capricorn.
- **Greasy skin:** when the Moon is waning and trine and, especially, sextile with the Sun (☽ △ ✳ ☉) – see pages 12-14. The skin will absorb the products a little less well but the cleansing action will be more effective. Perform during a waning Moon to help prevent dilation of the pores, making the skin firmer and more attractive.

Warts

To remove warts with the sap from plants such as greater celandine, marigold and the fig tree...

Start when the Moon is descending, preferably during the last quarter, and when it is in the superposition of the following signs and constellations:

- Leo/Leo (♌),
- Gemini/Taurus (♊)
(see pages 56-79)

Marigold

Celandine

48

Nails

For stronger nails, cut or file them when the Moon is waning and in an Earth or Air sign. Avoid the nodes.

Reduce the risk of in-growing nails by cutting them when the Moon is in the following signs: Leo, Virgo, Sagittarius, Capricorn and Aquarius, avoiding the lunar nodes.

Corns and callouses

Remove these when the Moon is waning and in the sign of Capricorn or Taurus. Another suitable time is when the Moon is waxing and in the sign of Virgo or Libra, though the effects are likely to be less successful.

Fasting

Fasting can be of great benefit to most people, but it is advisable to get permission from your doctor before embarking upon your first fast. Monitoring is essential for long fasts.

The New Moon is the best time to carry out a one-day fast, as your body will be cleansed more effectively. The New Moon is also a good time to begin fasts of up to a week. If you wish to fast for longer, begin when the Moon is descending and sextile with the Sun (☾ ✳ ☉) – see pages 12-14.

Detoxing

Start taking plants that help to detox your system through the liver when the Moon is in the sign of Virgo, and plants that work through the kidneys when it is in the sign of Libra. If possible, choose a time when the Moon is waning and sextile or trine with the Sun (☾ ✳ △ ☉) – see pages 12-14.

Treating worms

Carry out treatment to eradicate worms two or three days before the New Moon or, failing that, two or three days before the Full Moon.

Eating

Digestive problems ?

Key

Use your intuition to choose foods that most benefit you, and always eat in moderation.

A few pointers

- Meals should be eaten in a calm, relaxed atmosphere. Chew well and savour them to the full.
- Eat fruit and vegetables in season and grown locally (their energy is best adapted to our bodies).
- Give priority to vegetables (steamed or stir-fried in a wok) and fruit.
- Remember to eat sprouting seeds, seaweed, fibres, raw fruit (in between meals), and non-processed foods; use first cold pressed oils.

- Avoid combining starchy and protein foods in the same meal. Digesting them simultaneously makes conflicting demands on your stomach.
- Avoid in-between meals snacking, eat in moderation preserved meats, smoked products, soya beans and oats.
- If in doubt about a specific food, stop eating it for at least three weeks in order to monitor its effect on your body when you resume eating it.

Frequent issues

Excess of mucus: in order to help the liver when tired or stressed, limit or even avoid completely all dairy products.

Stomach acidity: meat and poorly-processed grains disrupt body equilibrium through acidification. Stress and lack of oxygen act similarly. Give priority to vegetables and in order to avoid deficiences, eat other foods in moderation.

Meals and the Moon
- When the Moon is waxing, nutrients are absorbed more easily.
- When the Moon is waxing and ascending, digestion requires less energy.
- People who suffer from constipation should avoid foods that contain little water (such as cereals) during Fire signs and the lunar nodes.

In order to conserve your vital energy, avoid the foods in the table below during the times indicated with letters (see p.10 and the calendar on pages 56-79). During those times, they take more energy to be digested properly, in particular for people with slow digestion.

Beef in sauce: c-f-g-o-u-w - Mutton in sauce: d-e-f-j-r-s-u - Pork in sauce: c-d-h-o-q-s-t - Poultry in sauce: b-i-j-q-r-s-u-v-w - Preserved meats: c-d-h-i-j-L-q-r-s-t-w-x-y - Oily fish: b-c-e-f-j-k-L-o-p-y - Smoked fish: a-b-c-d-h-i-j-k-L-o-p-q-u-v-y-z - Oysters and raw shellfish: h-m-n-r-u-v-y - Eggs: f-g-i-L-m-n-q-r-u-y - Dried beans: e-j-m-n-q-r-y - Lentils: b-c-e-m-n-q-s-y -Raw celeriac: i-j-k-l-q-w-y - Raw cabbages: c-d-i-j-m-n-v-w-x - Raw cauliflowers: e-f-g-h-m-n-o-q - Cucumbers, melons: b-c-d-f-s-t-u-v-w-y-z - Radishes: a-i-j-k-q-r-s-x - Salads (curly endive, escarole): e-i-j-k-L-m-n-r-s-y-z Raw tomatoes: b-i-m-n-o-q-r-y

How to use the calendar when living outside the United Kingdom

Times throughout the book are given in **Greenwich Mean Time** (28 October to 24 March) or **British Summer Time** (25 March to 27 October), as appropriate. **For those in the United Kingdom and Ireland, all times given, both summer and winter, are those shown on your watches.** The number of hours to take off or add on (if any) for other countries appear on the world map on the next two pages. Use these not only to calculate the right times but also the right periods of the day.

Let's take the example of the compost table from page 31, repeated below: a half colour bar appears on the afternoon of 7 March - this means afternoon in London, when it is evening (same day) in east Asia and morning (same day) in west America. So when you use tables like these, remember to take into consideration where you live to determine when to take benefits from the moon cycles.

COMPOST

	1	2	3	4	5	6	7	8	9	10	11	12	13	14	15	16	17	18	19	20	21	22	23	24	25	26	27	28	29	30	31
JANUARY					★			★															★	★	★★	★		★			
FEBRUARY	★	★		★									★★	★					★				★★	★					★		
MARCH	★		★									★★	★				★								★	★		★			
APRIL								★									★						★	★		★					
MAY					★★									★★	★						★		★								
JUNE		★★								★						★★				★								★★	★★		
JULY								★★	★								★						★★								★★
AUGUST	★			★★	★																	★★	★					★	★	★★	
SEPTEMBER										★										★					★	★	★★				
OCTOBER							★						★			★★	★						★	★	★★	★					
NOVEMBER							★												★	★	★	★	★★					★	★		
DECEMBER	★										★★						★	★	★★	★						★	★			★	
	1	2	3	4	5	6	7	8	9	10	11	12	13	14	15	16	17	18	19	20	21	22	23	24	25	26	27	28	29	30	31

(★) the more stars, the more favourable the day

■ a good time to add to or turn compost heaps that generate a high internal temperature (the majority of compost heaps)

□ choose these dates for working on slower acting compost heaps that generate less heat (often preferred by farmers and gardeners who practise biodynamics)

■ recommended for surface composting with non-rotted manure (broken down by worms);

▯ a vertical line dividing a date box indicates morning (left) or afternoon (right)

▬ a date box divided by a horizontal line indicates it is favourable for a certain type of composting (green for high temperature compost and orange for surface composting)

MANURE: spread manure when the Moon is descending, if possible on days marked orange (see the table above).

For tides, see page 80.

Calculating the time difference between where you live and London

Times throughout the book are given in **Greenwich Mean Time** (28 October to 24 March) or **British Summer Time** (25 March to 27 October), as appropriate. **For those in the United Kingdom and Ireland, all times given, both summer and winter, are those shown on your watches.** The number of hours to take off or add on for other countries appear in the map below – with some exceptions:

• USA and Canada: the switch to Daylight Saving Time (DST) does not happen on the same dates as in Europe — this means that between 11 and 25 March, as well as between 28 October and 4 November, you will need to reduce the time difference indicated on the map below by 1 hour.

• some countries do not observe Daylight Saving Time (DST), for instance Japan, Iceland, South Africa, Morocco, etc.: for these countries, use, the time difference as per the map below until 24 March and from 28 October, and use the same figure minus 1 hour between 25 March and 27 October.

• New Zealand: add 13 hours before 24 March and after 28 October, add 12 hours between 25 March and 1 April and also between 30 September and 27 October, and add 11 hours the rest of the time (from 2 April to 29 September)

Understanding the calendar

On the calendar on pages 56-79, the phases of the Moon (New Moon ●, first quarter ◖, last quarter ◗, Full Moon ○) as well as its perigee P and its apogee A, are represented in the top band.

The band beneath shows the Chinese seasons and inter-seasonal periods. Beneath these are the bands indicating the signs and constellations of the zodiac, each of which is illustrated by a coloured strip that corresponds to the four elements:

FIRE   EARTH   AIR   WATER

The letters between these bands indicate where signs and constellations can be used in conjunction (see page 10).

The curve of the coloured bands represents the Moon ascending and descending and the black triangles indicate when the change occurs. When the bands curve upwards, the Moon is ascending and vice versa. This movement is also reflected by the thin coloured bands beneath the wider blue band with the dates – green for the ascending Moon and yellow for the descending Moon.

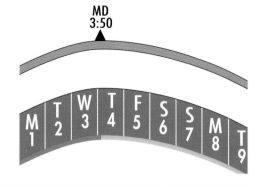

Cultivating the soil (particularly at depth), planting (for example, trees), planting out (especially plants with bare roots) and spreading compost or manure should be carried out when the Moon is descending, which is the best time for plants to take root.

The signs, letters and numbers in the white band are relevant to harvesting. The length of time is indicated by the vertical lines.

Ascending Moon:
harvest aerial parts of plant (green stars)
Descending Moon:
harvest parts of plant below ground (yellow stars)

The period for sowing different plants is indicated by the green band, which is in parallel with the constellations. The time when work should be carried out depends on why the plant is being grown (for its fruits, roots, flowers or leaves), avoiding the red zones. For example, choose a date favourable to 'leaf' plants for houseplants that do not flower and a 'flower' date for plants that do. Another example is to sow endives on 'root' dates and force their growth on 'leaf' dates.

The white band completes the information given in the green band. A summary of all the lunar and planetary effects on crops is given by indicating various zones ranging from 'harmful' (red band) to 'very favourable' (∗∗∗) and also 'to be avoided' (—). Use these symbols in conjunction with the green band above for a clear and comprehensive understanding.

All the times mentioned are Greenwich Mean Time or British Summer Time, as appropriate. For other countries, see page 80.
Cut out the detachable page giving instructions on how best to use the calendar and use it as a bookmark to remind you to use the calendar every month.

JANUARY

5 January: the Earth is at its closest to the Sun
(the perihelion)
– about 147 million km (92 million miles).

18 ♋ 26
07:31

10 ♈ 13
06:16

20:00

9
FM

25
09:

1
FQ

A
2

MD
21:47

CHINESE WINTER (WATER)

10:45 21:06

♈ ♉ ♊ ♋

0°21 12°11 24°06 6°11 18°27 0°59 13°49 04:36 26°54 10°15 23°51 09:45 7°37 21°32 13:29 5°34 19°39

18°30 0 22:17 j k l m n o p q r s t

g h i ♉ ♊ ♋ ♌ ♍ ♎

SIGNS

21:00 20:00 23:00 13:00 02:00

CONSTELLATIONS

S
1

M
2

T
3

W
4

T
5

F
6

S
7

S
8

M
9

T
10

W
11

T
12

F
13

S
14

S
15

M
16

HARVEST

21:00 21:00 14:00 20:00 23:00 13:00 02:00

CULTIVATION

Note: all times given are in Greenwich Mean Time.

To help you make full use of the calendar, activities are suggested for each month.

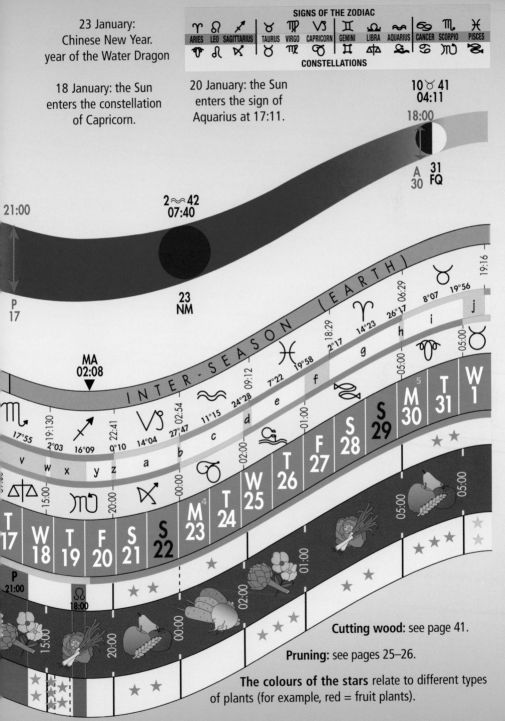

23 January:
Chinese New Year.
year of the Water Dragon

18 January: the Sun
enters the constellation
of Capricorn.

20 January: the Sun
enters the sign of
Aquarius at 17:11.

SIGNS OF THE ZODIAC

♈	♌	♐	♉	♍	♑	♊	♎	♒	♋	♏	♓
ARIES	LEO	SAGITTARIUS	TAURUS	VIRGO	CAPRICORN	GEMINI	LIBRA	AQUARIUS	CANCER	SCORPIO	PISCES

CONSTELLATIONS

10 ♉ 41
04:11

18:00

A 31
30 FQ

21:00

2 ♒ 42
07:40

P
17

23
NM

MA
02:08

INTER-SEASON (EARTH)

19:16

26°17   06:29   8°07   19:56

14°23

2°17   19°58   7°22   09:12   24°28   11°15   27°47   02:54   22:41   16°09   0°10

♈   g   h   i   j

♓   f   ♒   e   ♑   d   c   b   ♐   a   z   y   x   w   v

17°55   2°03   19:130   15:00   20:00   00:00   01:00   02:00   05:00   05:00   05:00

T   W   T   F   S   S   M⁴   T   W   T   F   S   S   M⁵   T   W
17   18   19   20   21   22   23   24   25   26   27   28   29   30   31   1

P
21:00

♋
18:00

15:00   20:00   00:00   02:00   01:00   05:00   05:00

Cutting wood: see page 41.

Pruning: see pages 25–26.

The colours of the stars relate to different types
of plants (for example, red = fruit plants).

57

FEBRUARY

SIGNS OF THE ZODIAC

♈	♌	♐	♉	♍	♑	♊	♎	♒	♋	♏	♓
ARIES	LEO	SAGITTARIUS	TAURUS	VIRGO	CAPRICORN	GEMINI	LIBRA	AQUARIUS	CANCER	SCORPIO	PISCES

CONSTELLATIONS

All the advice on the calendar also applies to **the southern hemisphere**, except for the inversion of the ascending and descending Moon (see page 4).

Note: all times given are in Greenwich Mean Time.

15 February: the Sun enters the constellation of Aquarius.

19 February: the Sun enters the sign of Pisces at 07:19.

10 ♊ 52
01:23

14:00

1
FQ

A
27

2 ♓ 42
22:36

MD
16:14

(W O O D)

21
NM

♉
16°00

♊
9°40

27°48

03:28

♈
10°16

22°18

4°11

14:31

j   k   L

i

♈
28°02

02:49

15°35

h

♉

g

2°55

17:32

♓

f

14:00

13:00

S P R I N G

♒

e

20°00

6°54

10:29

d

M
27⁹

T
28

W
29

T
1

♑

23°36

10°09

c

S
26

23:00

26°32

05:04

b

a

F
24

S
25

♏

W
23

T

♐

07:00

02:00

z

y

F
17

S
18

S
19

M
20⁸

T
21

W
22

T
23

13:00

14:00

6

02:00

07:00

11:00

10:00

11:00

Cereal crops: see page 35.

Hair care and depilation: see pages 46-47.

MARCH

SIGNS OF THE ZODIAC

ARIES	LEO	SAGITTARIUS	TAURUS	VIRGO	CAPRICORN	GEMINI	LIBRA	AQUARIUS	CANCER	SCORPIO	PISCES

CONSTELLATIONS

10 ♊ 52
01:23

1
FQ

18 ♍ 13
09:41

MD
16:14

10:00

24 ♐ 52
01:26

8
FM

P
10

15
LQ

MA
14:06

SIGNS

♊ 21°44 15:09 69 ♌ 13°22 ♍ 11°44 ♎ 11°12 ♏ 10°45 ♐ 9°31 23°27 7°07

CONSTELLATIONS

k   L 4°03 m 16°44 n 23:19 29°49 0:03:28 27°21 26°23 05:25 26°02 25°16 0:06:55 10:25

♉ 14:00 ♊ 18:00 69 07:00 ♌ 18:00 ♍ r s t u v w x y z a

HARVEST

| T 1 | F 2 | S 3 | S 4 | M 5 | T 6 | W 7 | T 8 | F 9 | S 10 | S 11 | M 12 | T 13 | W 14 | T 15 | F |

CULTIVATION

14:00   18:00   07:00   ♍ 21:00   ♎ 02:00   ♑ 07:00   ♐

P
10:00

18:00   21:00   21:00   02:00   07:00

March is a good month for **pruning** apple trees, but do not leave it any later.
Prune when the Moon is descending, for example from 2 to 14 March. See page 25.

11 March: the Sun enters the constellation of Pisces.

20 March: the Sun enters the sign of Aries at 06:16 (Vernal equinox).

To prevent onions and shallots from going to seed, plant them on a day favourable to 'root' plants when the Moon is descending, such as 9-11 March. When planting asparagus crowns, wait for a 'leaf' or roots date when the Moon is descending, such as 9-11-13am-14 March.

Note: all times given are in Greenwich Mean Time until 26 March. From 27 March, they are given in British Summer Time, thus taking into account the daylight saving change in the UK and Ireland.

APRIL

SIGNS OF THE ZODIAC

♈	♌	♐	♉	♍	♑	♊	♎	♒	♋	♏	♓
ARIES	LEO	SAGITTARIUS	TAURUS	VIRGO	CAPRICORN	GEMINI	LIBRA	AQUARIUS	CANCER	SCORPIO	PISCES

CONSTELLATIONS

For plants that easily go to seed
(lettuces, onions and so on), look for the appropriate constellation with the Moon in the descendent. For instance, 2-9pm-10pm April for lettuces.

Grafting: see page 26.

Weeds: see page 33.

18 April: the Sun enters the constellation of Aries.

19 April: the Sun enters the sign of Taurus at 18:13.

21 April: the beginning of the Red Moon.

1 ♉ 35
08:20   15:00

9 ♉ 29
10:59

A
22

21
NM

MD
06:38

29
FQ

INTER - SEASON   (EARTH)

Green manure: while waiting for the next food crop to grow, sow green manure to protect and enrich the soil (clover, phacelia, mustard, cereals with vetch or peas, buckwheat and spinach). Sow on a date favourable to 'leaf' plants to achieve abundant growth or, better still, a 'roots' date for maximum improvement to the structure of the soil.

14-15 April are good days for planting potatoes.

MAY

SIGNS OF THE ZODIAC

♈	♌	♐	♉	♍	♑	♊	♎	♒	♋	♏	♓
ARIES	LEO	SAGITTARIUS	TAURUS	VIRGO	CAPRICORN	GEMINI	LIBRA	AQUARIUS	CANCER	SCORPIO	PISCES

CONSTELLATIONS

13 May: the Sun
enters the constellation
of Taurus.

16 ♏ 01
04:36
05:00

22 ♒ 33
22:48

12
LQ

6 P
FM 6

MA
07:18

Good days for **sowing root vegetables**: 11-12 May.

20 May: end of the Red Moon.

20 May: the Sun enters the sign of Gemini at 17:17.

0 ♊ 21
00:48

17:00

7 ♍ 53
21:17

A
19

21
NM

MD
12:14

28
FQ

S U M M E R

(F I R E)

♉ 11:04 ♊ 12:32 ♋
24°02 5°52 17°39 29°00:06 11°18 23°13 5°15 17°29 23:12

h i j k l m n 29°53
27°32

o 12:33 ♌
p 25°07:07 ♍
q 8°51 22°33 11:47

♉ 10:00 11:00 18:00 r ♎
s 6°38 21°05 13:32
t

♋ 09:00 00:00 u
F 18 S 19 S 20 M 21 T 22 W 23 T 24 F 25 S 26 S 27 ♌

M 28 T 29 W 30 T 31 F 1

♉ 10:00

09:00 10:00 11:00 18:00 09:00 00:00

When sowing, always choose the constellation that suits the type
of plant, if possible when there is the maximum number of stars. For example,
8 May for leeks, 13-14 May for flowers. Always avoid the red zones and, as far as
possible, days marked with the sign (—).

Good days to **plant out flowers:** 23pm-24am May.

Note: all times given are in British Summer Time..

JUNE

SIGNS OF THE ZODIAC

ARIES LEO SAGITTARIUS | TAURUS VIRGO CAPRICORN | GEMINI LIBRA AQUARIUS | CANCER SCORPIO PISCES

CONSTELLATIONS

20 ♓ 54
11:42

14 ♐ 14
14:00   12:13

11
LQ

P
3   4
FM

MA
18:02

CHINESE

SIGNS

CONSTELLATIONS

HARVEST

CULTIVATION

Eclipses on 4 June : see page 8   **Hay**: see page 33.

20 June: the Sun enters the constellation of Gemini.

21 June: the Sun enters the sign of Cancer at 01:10 (Summer solstice).

28 ♊ 43
16:03

19
NM

MD
18:39

5 ♎ 54
04:31

19:00

SUMMER

06:25
26°20
8°11   18:35
20°08   2°14   14°30   26°57   26°04:48
9°37   22°31   12:44   5°39   19°03   18:16   2°42   16°39   21:33   9°52   23°05   29°56

j   k   l   m   n   o   p   q   r   s   t   u   v   w   x

♉   ♊   ♋   ♌   ♍   ♎   ♏

27
FQ

(FIRE)

P
1

S   L   T   W   T   F   S   S   M   T   W   T   F   S   S
17 18 19 20 21 22 23 24 25 26 27 28 29 30   1

16:00   17:00   17:00   23:00   15:00   06:00   19:03   16:39   06:00   13:00   19:00   23:05

25

17:00

26

07:00 19:00

16:00   17:00   23:00   15:00   06:00   13:00   P

Transplant during a descending moon. Even better, but not essential, would be to take into account the constellation.
For example, for leeks, on a 'leaf' date such as the 4-22-23am June

Pick horsetail when the Moon is ascending and in an Earth constellation, for instance 7pm-8-9am-17pm-18 June, to dry it for future use. See page 30.

To ensure grass grows back more slowly, cut it on a date favourable to 'flower' plants or, if that is not possible, when the Moon is descending, for instance 1-2-19-20-21-26-27-28-29am June.

JULY

SIGNS OF THE ZODIAC

| ♈ | ♌ | ♐ | ♉ | ♍ | ♑ | ♊ | ♎ | ♒ | ♋ | ♏ | ♓ |
| ARIES | LEO | SAGITTARIUS | TAURUS | VIRGO | CAPRICORN | GEMINI | LIBRA | AQUARIUS | CANCER | SCORPIO | PISCES |

CONSTELLATIONS

5 July: the earth is at its furthest
from the Sun
(its aphelion) – about
152 million km (95 million miles).

18:00

19 ♈ 11
02:49

A
13

19:00

12 ♑ 14
19:53

MD
02:18

11
LQ

S U M M E R

13:28

♉

22°53   4°42   16°37

♊

11°05

00:32

♈

17°15   29°14   i   j   k

P
1

3
FM

g   h

5°02

23:00

♉

13:15

00:00

MA
04:32

C H I N E S E

13°15   22°31

f

♓

9°38   05:30

e

♒

26°20

d

12°38

c

21:00

SIGNS

♐

23:52

♑

01:27

b

14°42   29°27   14°06   28°32

23:00

♊

x   y   z   a   ♋

22:00

CONSTELLATIONS

♍♏

21:00

♐

22:00

♊

♋

S
1

M
2

T
3

W
4

T
5

F
6

S
7

S
8

M
9

T
10

W
11

T
12

F
13

S
14

S
15

M
16

27   28

23:00

00:00

HARVEST

♋ P
07:00 19:00

21:00

23:00

21:00

23:00

CULTIVATION

21:00

22:00

21:00

Note: all times given are in British Summer Time.

Good days to plant out strawberries: 21-22 July.

19 July: the Sun enters the constellation of Cancer.

22 July: the Sun enters the sign of Leo at 12:02.

26 ♋ 55
05:25

19
NM

3 ♏ 47
09:57

10:00

26
FQ

P
29

MA
13:15

(F I R E)

♋

10°59   11:14   23:31

n

♌

o   6°17   19°18   18:25

p

♍

q   2°32   15°59   23:39

r

♎

s   29°37   13°25   27°22

t   03:30

♏

u   11°26   25°39   06:19

v   9°56

♐

w   24°18   08:30

x

♑

y   8°39   22°56   10:57

z   a   b   c

I N T E R - S E A S O N   (E A R T H)

T 7
W 18
T 19
F 20
S 21
S 22
L 23
T 24
W 25
T 26
F 27
S 28
S 29
M 30
T 31
W 1

30

31

06:00   21:00   12:00   19:00   02:00   05:00   08:00

♍

♎ △ △ ♎   ♍♑

♐

♋
12:00   P 10:00

Water plants more during
dry periods – to ensure roots
grow deep, water generously but less
often, rather than little and often. To avoid
water evaporating too quickly, hoe the ground a
few hours after watering, if possible in the evening with a
waxing Moon in an Earth or Water sign, e.g. 3-21-22-23-26-27 July.

AUGUST

10 August: the Sun enters the constellation of Leo.

Take cuttings from geraniums: preferably when the Moon is ascending on a day favourable to 'flower' plants, for example, 3-4 August. Take the cutting from a healthy stem just below a leaf joint. Start the cutting off in a little peat or water; and when rooted, plant in soil-based compost.

Shield budding: see page 26.

70

SIGNS OF THE ZODIAC

♈	♌	♐	♉	♍	♑	♊	♎	♒	♋	♏	♓
ARIES	LEO	SAGITTARIUS	TAURUS	VIRGO	CAPRICORN	GEMINI	LIBRA	AQUARIUS	CANCER	SCORPIO	PISCES

CONSTELLATIONS

22 August: the Sun enters
the sign of Virgo at 19:08.

♌ 08
:56

8 ♓ 34
14:59

20:00 1 ♐ 48
14:55

31
FM

P   24
23   FQ

AUTUMN

28°33 01:34

♍ 12°11

26°03 05:46

q

♎ 10°04

r

24°09 08:55

MA
19:45
▼

(M E T A L)

s

18:00

t

♏ 8°17

22°25 11:51

u

♐

15:00

♑

18°37

2°29 18:40

16°12

23:32

29°42

12°56

f

6°32 20°38 4°40

♒

b   c   d   e

14:00

17:00

♌

v   w   x   y   z   a

♋

S
18

S
19

M
20

T
21

♍

01:00

♎

07:00

W
22

T
23

F
24

♑

12:00

S
25

S
26

♐

16:00

M
27

T
28

W
29

T
30

F
31

S
1

P
20:00

♋
13:00

18:00

01:00

07:00

12:00

16:00

17:00

14:00

Note: all times given are in
British Summer Time.

Disbud chrysanthemums when the Moon is in the sign of Libra, for example 23 August.

71

SEPTEMBER

15 September: the Sun enters the constellation of Virgo.

Compost: apply compost on one of the dates given on page 31.
Wait for the a descending Moon before applying.
For **spreading manure**: see page 31.

Cereal crops: see page 35.

72

SIGNS OF THE ZODIAC

ARIES	LEO	SAGITTARIUS	TAURUS	VIRGO	CAPRICORN	GEMINI	LIBRA	AQUARIUS	CANCER	SCORPIO	PISCES

CONSTELLATIONS

22 September: the Sun enters
the sign of Libra at 16:50.
(Autumnal equinox)

7 ♈ 22
04:20

37
12

04:00

0 ♑ 12
20:42

30
FM

P
19

22
FQ

MA
01:09

13:56

5°24   19°51   15:47

♎   ♏   ♐   ♑   ♒   ♓   ♈   g

t   4°22   18°51   17:35   3°13   17°28   1°32   20:22   15°25   29°06   00:34   12°37   25°55   06:25   9°02   21°55   14:15   4°35   17°01

♍   u   v   w   x   y   z   a   b   c   d   e   f

M   S   S
1   30   29

S   M   T   W   T   F   S   S   M   T   W   T   F   S   S   M
6   17   18   19   20   21   22   23   24   25   26   27   28   29   30   1

P
04:00

♌
14:00

07:00   13:00   17:00   21:00   22:00   00:00

Preserving fruit: take
account of the 'harvest' band
when picking fruit and also of the
information on page 27.

Note: all times given are in British Summer Time.

73

OCTOBER

♈	♌	♐	♉	♍	♑	♊	♎	♒	♋	♏	♓
ARIES	LEO	SAGITTARIUS	TAURUS	VIRGO	CAPRICORN	GEMINI	LIBRA	AQUARIUS	CANCER	SCORPIO	PISCES

CONSTELLATIONS

02:00

A 5

15 ♋ 26
08:34

8
LQ

22 ♎ 32
13:04

15
NM

MD
02:45

C H I N E S E   A U T U M N   (M E T A L)

SIGNS

♈ 00:27
29°15

♉
12:48
16°47

♊
01:46
28°38

♋
12:56
5°17

♌
18:09
20:25
1°28

♍
15°13
00:03
29°22

♎
13:54
01:07
28°41

g   h   i   11°18   j   23°12   k   l   5°00   m   n   10°36   22°47   o   p   q   r   s   t   u

23:00   23:00   00:00   07:00   23:00   12:00

CONSTELLATIONS

M 1   T 2   W 3   T 4   F 5   S 6   S 7   M 8   T 9   W 10   T 11   F 12   S 13   S 14   L 15   T 16

40   06:00   ♉   41   42

♏

HARVEST

23:00   23:00   00:00   07:00   23:00   12:00   16:00

CULTIVATION

Note: all times given are in British Summer Time until 29 October and GMT from 30 October.

Cuttings: cut on the evening of the 5th (end of the ascending moon) and plant them on the morning of the 6th (beginning of the descending moon).

74

23 October: the Sun enters the sign of Scorpio at 02:15.

31 October: the Sun enters the constellation of Libra.

15:00

6 ♉ 48
19:51

A
1

29 FM

29 ♑ 09
04:33

22 FQ

INTER-SEASON (EARTH)

♉ 19:41 ♊

MA
07:43

♓ 20:32 ♈ 13°37 26°20 07:16 8°22 20°17 05:00
1°17 18°43 26°07:16

g h i j k

≈ 12:01 5°55 f ♒ 05:00 ♉
22°53 e

♑ 06:03 9°34 d 04:00
25°57

c ♈

01:27 ♐ 02:42 ♑ 12°01 b ♎ 05:00
28°29 13°15 27°46 05:00

a ♉ 08 11:00
03:00

w x y z

21:00 ♍ 00:00 ♐ 05:00
09:00

T F S S M 43 T W T F S S M 44 T W T
18 19 20 21 22 23 24 25 26 27 28 29 30 31 1

75

SIGNS OF THE ZODIAC

♈	♌	♐	♉	♍	♑	♊	♎	♒	♋	♏	♓
ARIES	LEO	SAGITTARIUS	TAURUS	VIRGO	CAPRICORN	GEMINI	LIBRA	AQUARIUS	CANCER	SCORPIO	PISCES

CONSTELLATIONS

15:00

A
1

15 ♉ 00
00:37

7
LQ

MD
08:17 ▲

21 ♏ 57
22:09
10:00

13 P
NM 14

INTER-SEASON (EARTH)

CHINESE

SIGNS

♊ 08:44
13°54 25°41   7°32 19°31 ♋ 1°42 14°10 05:36 26°57

CONSTELLATIONS

k L m   n   o   p   q   ♍ 10°10

HARVEST

♉   -06:00   ♊   -14:00   ♋   -06:00   r   23°49 10:36 ♎ 7°55 22°28 12:11 ♏ 7°22 22°28 13:53 ♐ 7°39

T   F   S   S   M   T   W   T   F   S   S   M   T   W   T
1   2   3   4   5   6   7   8   9   10 11 12 13 14 1.

♌   ♍   s   t   u   v   w   x
-22:00   -02:00   -07:00

CULTIVATION

06:00   14:00   06:00   22:00

♉
05:00 P
10:00

02:00

07:00

Planting trees: see page 25.

Preserving root vegetables: make sure you
look for the zones containing two yellow stars in the
'harvest' line, for example, 2-7-8-9-10-11-12 November.

Timber: cut timber on the dates marked on page 41 to benefit from the
lunar influences, if possible during November and December to benefit from
the descending Sun as well.

19 November: the Sun enters the constellation of Scorpio.

21 November: the Sun enters the sign of Sagittarius at 22:51.

6 ♊ 47
14: 47 20:00

28 A
FM 28

28 ♒ 41
14:33

MD
14:32

20
FQ

(W A T E R)

♉   ♊   ♋
        29°00:59 10°48 22°37   4°29
5°18 17°11   29°00   13:56
        12:19
♈
23°20   i   j   k   L   m   n
11°11
♓   h   ♉
28°51 16°14   g   11:00   ♊
3°19 16:14   11:00   12:00
W I N T E R   f
~~~~   e 9:00
6°18 20°01
22°10   d
12:11
♑
7°38   c
        b
♐   a
        09:00

S   S   M   T   W   T   F   S
17   18   19   20   21   22   23   24

M   48   M   T   W   T   F   S
25   26   27   28   29   30   1

♉
17:00

★ ★

Eclipses on 13 November: see page 8.

Note: all times given are in Greenwich Mean Time.

77

DECEMBER

SIGNS OF THE ZODIAC

ARIES	LEO	SAGITTARIUS	TAURUS	VIRGO	CAPRICORN	GEMINI	LIBRA	AQUARIUS	CANCER	SCORPIO	PISCES

CONSTELLATIONS

14 ♍ 55
15:33

6
LQ

21 ♐ 45
23:00 08:43

SIGNS

♋ 16°25 28°30 04:58

CONSTELLATIONS

n ♉ 10°44 23°12 11:53

o

p ♍ 5°57 19:01 18:36

q

r 2:29 ♎ 16°23

s 21:52 0°41 ♏ 15°23 22:23

t ♐ 15°35 21:44 ♑ 15°53 21:54

u 0°23 21:48 0°39

v w x y z a b

P 13
13 NM

MA
03:42 ▼

HARVEST

S 1 S 2 M 3 49 T 4 13:00 W 5 T 6 F 7 S 8 S 9 M 10 50 T 11 W 12 T 13 F 14 S 15 S 1

♌ 06:00 ♍ ♏ ♎ 13:00 18:00

CULTIVATION

20:00 13:00 06:00 13:00

⚏ 16:00 P 23:00 13:00 18:00 19:00 19:00 19:00

For timber: see page 41.

Cut **firewood** when the Moon is descending from 1 to 12 and from 27 to 31 December.

19 December: the Sun enters the constellation of Sagittarius.

21 December: the Sun enters the sign of Capricorn at 12:13.

The period between Christmas and Epiphany is a good time for people to **reflect and take stock**. You can also make use of this time to try and predict what the weather will be like during the next 12 months. Make a very precise note at fixed hours several times a day of what the weather is like between 24 December and 6 January.

In theory, the weather in January will correspond to the weather as it was on 24/25 December, the weather in February to the weather conditions on 25/26 December and so on. Keep 24/25 December as your starting point. Try it and see if it works.

Influence of tides... where you live

The influence of tides (see page 16) naturally depends on the tides nearest to where you live. Tide effects described in this book are valid in the United Kingdom and Ireland as detailed on page 16: in those islands, no one lives very far from the sea!

If you wish to take into consideration the influence of tides in your local area (assuming you do live not too far inland), you will need to consult local tide tables, which should be easily found on the internet.

Using the calendar made easy

This diagram provides a clearer, simpler version of the information contained in the tear-out section. This information is a summary of our interpretation of the various lunar and planetary influences.

Descending Moon: the band descends and the line is yellow

Between the New Moon and the Full Moon, the Moon is waxing.

Ascending Moon: the band ascends and the line is green

Avoid the red zones and the symbol (—)

Harvesting band

Green stars = harvest aerial plant parts

Yellow stars = harvest plant parts below ground

The more stars there are, the more suitable the day is for sowing or cultivating the crop represented by the symbols

Cultivation band
The colour of the stars corresponds to the different types of crop

fruit = ★

root = ★

flower = ★

leaf = ★

The note pages

Times of moon rising (blue) and setting (black) [p.17]

Date

Moon phases [p.2]

Ascending (green) and descending (yellow) moon [p.4]

Constellations (cultures) [p.10]
see the calendar [p.56 to 79]

Tide effects [p.16]. Times in green: show the beginning of the effect of the rising tide, those in black: show the beginning of the effect of the receding tide.
Green zone: period of rising tide influence, for example from 12:00 (start) to 17:45 (end).
White zone: period of receding tide influence, for example from 05:15 (start) to 12:00 (end).

Space for your notes

JANUARY

Date	Moon rise/set		Moon	Tide/Constellation
S 1	06:16	01:15 / 06:45		
	00:14 / 11:12	12:15		
		19:15 ★		W.1
M 2	WAXING	02:15 / 07:30		
		12:30	20:00 / A / 21:00	
	01:20 / 11:33	20:00		
T 3	WAXING	03:30 / 08:15		
		13:00 ★		
	02:26 / 11:56	20:45 ★		
W 4		04:30 / 09:00 ★		
		13:30		
	03:30 / 12:25	21:30	21:00	
T 5		05:30 / 09:45 ★		
		14:00 ★		
	04:33 / 13:00	22:15		
F 6	21:47	06:30 / 10:45		
	WAXING	14:45 ♋		
	05:32 / 13:44	23:00	14:00	
S 7	WAXING	07:30 / 11:30 ⋯		
		15:45 —		
	06:25 / 14:38		20:00 ♋ ☿ 21:00	
S 8		00:00 / 08:15 ★		
		12:30 ★		
	07:10 / 15:41	16:45 ★		W.2
M 9	07:31	00:45 / 08:45 ★		
		13:15 ★		
	07:47 / 16:50	17:45	23:00	
T 10	WANING	01:45 / 09:15 ★		
		14:00 ★		
	08:18 / 18:04	19:00 ★		

81

W 11
08:45 / 19:20
02:30
09:45
★ ★★
13:00
15:00
20:15

T 12
09:08 / 20:38
03:15
10:15 ★
15:45
21:45 ★

WANING

F 13
09:29 / 21:56
04:15
10:30
16:30
23:00 / 02:00

S 14
09:50 / 23:15
05:00
10:45
17:30 ★

S 15
10:12
00:15
05:45 ★
11:15 ★
18:15
— W.3

09:09

M 16
00:34 / 10:38
01:30
06:45 ★
11:45 ★
19:15 ★ ★

T 17
01:54 / 11:08
03:00
07:30 / 09:00
12:15
P
20:00 / 21:00

W 18
03:13 / 11:46
04:15
08:30 ★
12:45 ★ / 15:00
21:00

T 19
04:26 / 12:33
05:30 ★
09:30 ★
13:30
22:00 / 18:00

02.08 WANING

F 20
05:29 / 13:32
06:30
10:30
14:30 / 20:00
23:00

S 21
06:21 / 14:41
07:15
11:30
15:45 ★

S 22
07:02 / 15:55
00:00
08:00 ★
12:30
17:00 / 00:00
— W.

07:40

M 23
07:34 / 17:11
00:45
08:30
13:15
18:15

JANUARY

T 24	07:59 / 18:26	01:45 · 09:00 · 14:00 · 19:30 — 02:00
W 25	08:21 / 19:38	02:30 · 09:15 · 15:00 ★ · 20:45 ★
T 26	08:41 / 20:48	03:15 · 09:45 ★ · 15:45 · 21:45 — 01:00
F 27	08:59 / 21:57	04:00 · 10:00 · 16:15 · 23:00
S 28	09:17 / 23:04	04:45 ★ · 10:15 ★ · 17:00 ★
S 29	09:37	00:00 / 05:30 · 10:30 · 17:45
M 30	00:10 / 10:00	01:15 · 06:15 · 11:00 ★★ · 18:30 A — 05:00 / 18:00
T 31	01:15 / 10:26	02:15 / 07:00 ★ · 11:30 ★ · 19:15 ★

WAXING

W.5

FEBRUARY

W 1	02:18 / 10:58	03:15 / 07:45 · 12:00 · 20:00 ★ — 05:00
T 2	03:18 / 11:37	04:15 ★ · 08:30 · 12:30 · 21:00 ♋ — 20:00
F 3	04:14 / 12:26	05:15 ★ · 09:15 ★ · 13:30 · 21:45 ★
S 4	05:02 / 13:24	06:00 · 10:15 · 14:30 ★ · 22:45 ★ — 04:00
S 5	05:43 / 14:31	06:45 · 11:00 ★ · 15:30 ★ · 23:30

WAXING

04:11

07:12

83

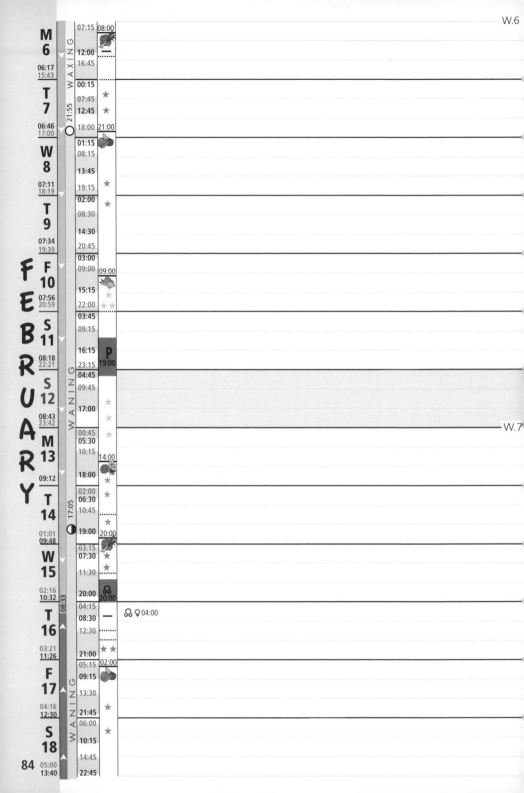

W.7

FEBRUARY

M 6	07:15	08:00
	12:00	
06:17 15:43	16:45	
T 7	00:15	★
	07:45	★
	12:45	
06:46 17:00	18:00	21:00
W 8	01:15	
	08:15	
	13:45	
07:11 18:19	19:15	★
T 9	02:00	★
	08:30	
	14:30	
07:34 19:39	20:45	
F 10	03:00	09:00
	09:00	
	15:15	★
07:56 20:59	22:00	★ ★
S 11	03:45	
	09:15	
	16:15	P
08:18 22:21	23:15	19:00
S 12	04:45	
	09:45	
	17:00	★
08:43 23:42		★
M 13	00:45 05:30	★
	10:15	14:00
	18:00	★
09:12		
T 14	02:00 06:30	★
	10:45	
		★
01:01 09:48	19:00	20:00
W 15	03:15 07:30	★
	11:30	★
	20:00	☊ 20:00
02:16 10:32		
T 16	04:15	—
	08:30	☊ ♀ 04:00
	12:30	
03:21 11:26	21:00	★ ★
F 17	05:15	02:00
	09:15	
	13:30	
04:16 12:30	21:45	★
S 18	06:00	
	10:15	★
	14:45	
05:00 13:40	22:45	

WAXING 21:55 ○

WANING 17:05 ◑

08:33

WANING

F E B R U A R Y

S **19**	06:30	07:00		
	11:15	—		
	16:00	★		
05:34 14:54	23:30			W.8
M **20**	07:00	★	WANING	
	12:00	★		
	17:15	★		
06:02 16:08	00:30			
T **21**	07:30	11:00	22:36 ●	
	12:45			
	18:15	★		
06:25 17:20	01:15			
W **22**	07:45	★		
	13:30			
	19:30	★		
06:45 18:31	02:00			
T **23**	08:00	10:00	WAXING	
	14:15			
07:04 19:40	20:45			
F **24**	02:30			
	08:30			
	15:00	★		
07:23 20:47	21:45			
S **25**	03:15			
	08:45			
	15:45			
07:42 21:54	23:00			
S **26**	04:00	—		
	09:00	13:00 ☊ ☿14:00		
	16:30	—		W.9
08:04 23:00	00:00	★		
M **27**	04:45	★★	WAXING	
	09:30	A 14:00		
	17:15	★		
08:29	01:00	★		
T **28**	05:30	14:00		
	10:00			
	18:00			
00:04 08:58	02:00	★		
W **29**	06:15	★		
	10:30			
	18:45	23:00 ☿	01:23 ◗	
01:05 09:34	03:00			
T **1**	07:15	....	16:14 WAXING	
	11:15	★		
02:01 10:18	19:30	★		
F **2**	03:45			
	08:00	14:00		
02:52 11:10	12:15			
	20:30			

85

MARCH

S 3	04:30	
	08:45	
03:35	13:15	★
12:12	21:15	★
S 4	05:15	★
	09:45	
	14:15	18:00
04:12	22:15	
13:20		
M 5	05:45	
	10:30	★
WAXING	15:30	★
04:44	23:00	
14:34	06:15	07:00
T 6	11:30	
05:11	16:45	
15:52	23:45	
W 7	06:30	★
	12:15	★
05:35	18:15	★
17:12	00:45	
T 8	07:00	
09:41 ○	13:15	★ ★
05:58	19:30	18:00
18:34		
F 9	01:30	
	07:15	★
06:21	14:00	★
19:58	21:00	★
S 10	02:30	**P**
	07:45	
06:46	15:00	10:00
21:22	22:15	
S 11	03:30	★
WANING	08:15	★
07:14	15:45	★
22:45	23:45	21:00
M 12	04:15	
	08:45	★
07:49	16:45	★
	01:00	02:00
T 13	05:15	
	09:30	★ ★
00:03	17:45	★
08:31		○ 21:00
14:06	02:15	
W 14	06:15	★
	10:30	★
01:26	18:45	★
01:13	03:15	07:00
09:23		
◑		
T 15	07:15	
	11:30	
86	19:45	★
02:12		
10:25		

W.10

W.11

Day	Times		
F 16	04:00		
	08:15	★	
	12:30		
02:59 / 11:33	20:45	★	
S 17	04:30	★	
	09:00		
	13:45	13:00	
03:35 / 12:45	21:30	★	
	05:00		
S 18	10:00	★	
	15:00	★	
04:05 / 13:57	22:15	★	W.12
M 19	05:30		
	10:45		
	16:15	17:00	
04:29 / 15:08	23:00		
T 20	05:45		
	11:30		
	17:15	★	
04:50 / 16:18	23:45	★	
W 21	06:15		
	12:15	17:00	
05:10 / 17:27	18:30		
	00:30	★	
T 22	06:30	★	
	13:00	★	
05:28 / 18:34	19:30		
F 23	01:15		
	06:45		
	13:45		
05:48 / 19:41	20:45		
S 24	02:00		
	07:15		
	14:15		
06:09 / 20:47	21:45	20:00	
S 25	03:45		
	08:30	★	
	16:00	★	
07:33 / 22:51	23:45	★	W.13
M 26	04:30	A / 07:00	
	09:00	★	
	16:45	★	
08:00 / 23:53		22:00	
T 27	01:00		
	05:15		
	09:30	★	
	17:45	★	
08:34		01:00	
W 28	01:45		
	06:00		
	10:15	★	
00:51 / 09:14	18:30	★	

WANING

14:38

WAXING

APRIL

Day	Times		
W 11	02:00 / **06:15** / 10:15		★ ★ ★
			15:00
01:02 / **09:15**	**18:45**		
T 12	03:00 / **07:00** / 11:30		★ ★
01:55 / **10:23**	**19:30**		
F 13	03:30 / **08:00** / 12:30	11:51	★
			20:00
02:36 / **11:36**	**20:30**		
S 14	04:15 / **09:00** / 13:45		
03:08 / **12:49**	**21:15**		★ ★
S 15	04:30 / **09:45** / 15:00		★
03:34 / **14:00**	**22:00**	00:00	W.16
M 16	05:00 / **10:30** / 16:15		
03:56 / **15:10**	**22:45**		★
T 17	05:15 / **11:15** / 17:15		★
04:16 / **16:18**	**23:30**	00:00	
W 18	05:30 / **12:00** / 18:30		★
04:34 / **17:25**			
T 19	00:15 / **06:00** / 12:30		★ ★
04:54 / **18:31**	**19:30**		
F 20	01:00 / **06:15** / 13:15		
05:14 / **19:37**	**20:30**	03:00	
S 21	01:45 / **06:30** / **14:00**	08:20	
05:37 / **20:42**	21:45		★
S 22	02:30 / **07:00** / **14:45**		★ ★
		A 15:00	
06:03 / **21:45**	22:45		★ ★ W.17
M 23	03:15 / **07:30** / 15:30	04:00	★
06:35 / **22:44**	23:45		

WANING — WANING — WAXING — WAXING

89

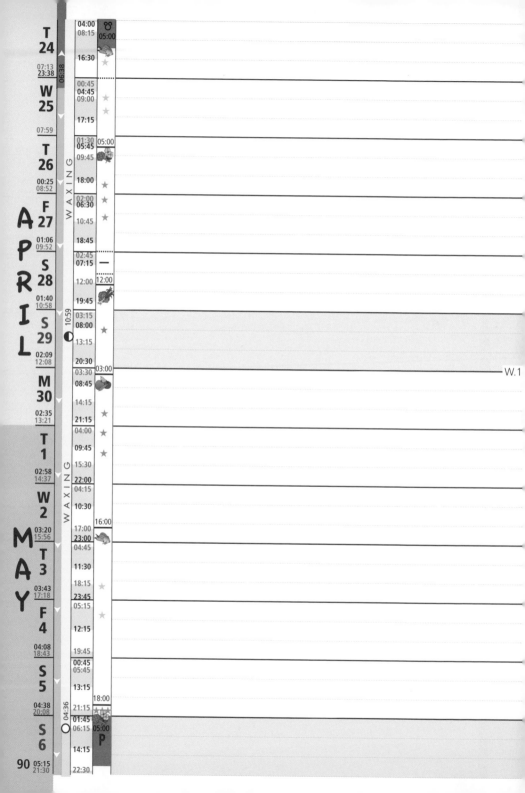

APRIL

T 24	04:00 / 08:15	05:00
	16:30	
07:13 / 23:38		
W 25	00:45 / 04:45 / 09:00	
	17:15	
07:59		
T 26	01:30 / 05:45 / 09:45	05:00
	18:00	
00:25 / 08:52		
F 27	02:00 / 06:30 / 10:45	
	18:45	
01:06 / 09:52		
S 28	02:45 / 07:15 / 12:00	12:00
	19:45	
01:40 / 10:58		
S 29	03:15 / 08:00 / 13:15	
	20:30	
02:09 / 12:08		
M 30	03:30 / 08:45 / 14:15	03:00
	21:15	W. 1
02:35 / 13:21		

WAXING

06:38

10:59

MAY

T 1	04:00 / 09:45 / 15:30	
	22:00	
02:58 / 14:37		
W 2	04:15 / 10:30 / 17:00	
	23:00	16:00
03:20 / 15:56		
T 3	04:45 / 11:30 / 18:15	
	23:45	
03:43 / 17:18		
F 4	05:15 / 12:15 / 19:45	
04:08 / 18:43		
S 5	00:45 / 05:45 / 13:15	
	21:15	18:00
04:38 / 20:08		
S 6	01:45 / 06:15 / 14:15	05:00
	22:30	P
05:15 / 21:30		

WAXING

04:36

M **7**	2:45 7:00	♌
06:01 22:43	15:15 **11:00**	
	23:45	
T **8**	3:45 8:00	★ ★
06:58 23:44	16:15	★
	00:00	
W **9**	0:45 **5:00** 9:00	
08:05	17:30	★
T **10**	1:30 **5:45** 10:15	★
00:31 **09:19**	18:15	
F **11**	2:15 **6:45** 11:30	03:00
01:08 **10:34**	19:15	★
S **12**	2:30 **7:45** 12:45	★ ★
01:37 **11:49**	**20:00**	
S **13**	3:00 8:30 14:00	06:00
02:00 **13:00**	**20:45**	★
M **14**	3:15 9:15 15:15	★
02:21 **14:09**	**21:30**	
T **15**	3:45 10:00 16:15	06:00
02:41 **15:17**	**22:15**	
W **16**	4:00 10:30 17:30	★ ★
03:00 **16:23**	**23:00**	
T **17**	4:15 11:15 18:30	★
03:19 **17:29**	**23:45**	
F **18**	4:45 12:00 19:30	09:00
03:41 **18:34**		★
S **19**	0:30 5:00 12:45	★
04:07 **19:37**	20:30	**A** 17:00 ★★

07:18

WANING

22:48

WANING

W.20

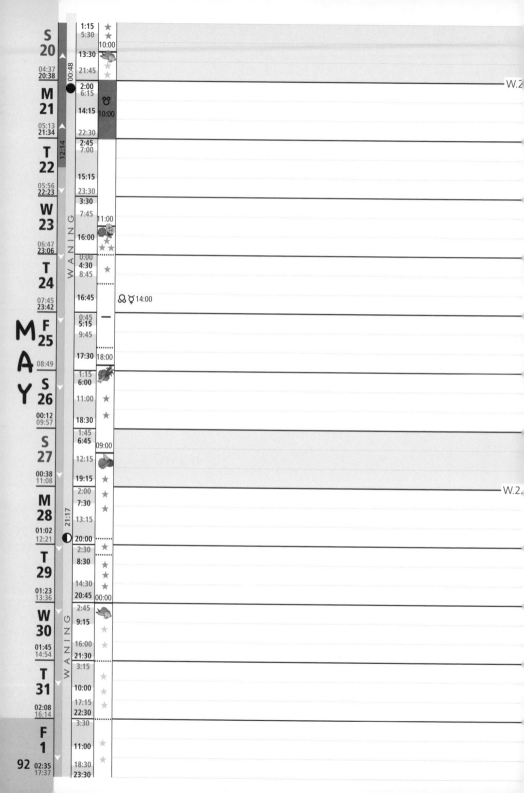

MAY

S 20 04:37 / 20:38	00:48 ●	1:15 ⭐ / 5:30 ⭐ / 10:00 / 13:30 🐢 / 21:45 ⭐
M 21 05:13 / 21:34	12:14	2:00 / 6:15 ♉ / 14:15 10:00 / 22:30
T 22 05:56 / 22:23		2:45 / 7:00 / 15:15 / 23:30
W 23 06:47 / 23:06	W A N I N G	3:30 / 7:45 11:00 / 16:00 🦀 / ⭐⭐
T 24 07:45 / 23:42		0:00 / 4:30 / 8:45 ⭐ / 16:45 ☊ ☿ 14:00
M F 25 08:49		0:45 / 5:15 — / 9:45 / 17:30 18:00
A Y S 26 00:12 / 09:57		1:15 / 6:00 🦀 / 11:00 ⭐ / 18:30 ⭐
S 27 00:38 / 11:08		1:45 / 6:45 09:00 / 12:15 🍇 / 19:15 ⭐
M 28 01:02 / 12:21	21:17 ◑	2:00 ⭐ / 7:30 ⭐ / 13:15 / 20:00 ⭐
T 29 01:23 / 13:36		2:30 ⭐ / 8:30 ⭐ / 14:30 ⭐ / 20:45 00:00
W 30 01:45 / 14:54	W A N I N G	2:45 🐢 / 9:15 ⭐ / 16:00 ⭐ / 21:30
T 31 02:08 / 16:14		3:15 ⭐ / 10:00 ⭐ / 17:15 ⭐ / 22:30
F 1 02:35 / 17:37		3:30 / 11:00 ⭐ / 18:30 ⭐ / 23:30

W.2

W.2

JUNE

S 2	4:00	05:00
	12:00	★
3:07 / 19:00	20:00	★
		★
S 3	0:30 / 4:45	09:00
	13:00	14:00
3:47 / 20:18	21:15	22:00
M 4	1:30 / 5:45	
	14:00	★
4:38 / 21:26	22:30	★
T 5	2:30 / 6:45	★ ★★ 11:00
	15:00	
5:41 / 22:21	23:15	★
W 6	3:30 / 8:00	★
	16:00	— ☊ ♀ 18:00
6:54 / 23:04		
T 7	0:00 / 4:30 / 9:15	★ 12:00
	17:00	
8:11 / 23:37		
F 8	0:30 / 5:30	★
	10:30	★
9:29	18:00	★
S 9	1:00 / 6:15	
	11:45	14:00
0:03 / 10:44	18:45	
S 10	1:30 / 7:00	★
	13:00	
0:26 / 11:56	19:30	★
M 11	1:45 / 7:45	12:00
	14:00	
0:46 / 13:05	20:15	
T 12	2:00 / 8:30	
	15:15	★
1:05 / 14:13	21:00	
W 13	2:30 / 9:15	★
	16:15	★
1:25 / 15:19	21:30	
T 14	2:45 / 10:00	
	17:30	16:00
1:46 / 16:24	22:15	

WAXING

12:13 18:02 ○

WANING

11:42 ◑

W.23

W.24

T 28	01:30 08:45	
00:37 / 15:16	16:15 ★ 21:15 ★	
F 29	02:00 09:45	13:00
01:05 / 16:36	17:30 22:15 ★	
S 30	02:45 ★ 10:45 ★	
01:40 / 17:54	19:00 23:15	19:00
S 1	03:30 ♋ 07:00 11:45	
02:25 / 19:06	20:00 **P** 19:00	♉ ☿ 21:00 — W.27 —
M 2	00:15 04:15 12:45 ★ ★	
03:21 / 20:07	21:00	21:00
T 3	01:15 05:30 13:45 ★ ★ ★	
04:28 / 20:55	22:00	
W 4	02:15 06:45 14:45 —	
05:43 / 21:33	22:30	22:00
T 5	03:15 08:00 15:45 ★	
07:02 / 22:04	23:00 ★	
F 6	04:00 ★ 09:15 16:30	
08:20 / 22:29	23:30	23:00
S 7	05:00 10:30 17:15 ★	
09:35 / 22:50	23:45 05:45 ★	
S 8	11:45	
10:48 / 23:10	18:00	21:00 — W.28 —
M 9	00:15 06:30 13:00 ★	
11:58 / 23:30	18:45 ★	
T 10	00:30 07:15 ★ 14:00	
13:05 / 23:51	19:30	

WAXING

WANING

04:32

19:53

95

W 11	00:45 / 08:00 / 15:15 / 20:15	02:49 ◐ · 23:00 · ★ ★ ★★ ★★
14:12		
T 12	01:15 / 08:45 / 16:15 / 21:00	★
00:14 / 15:17		
F 13	01:45 / 09:30 / 17:15 / 21:45	★ · 18:00 · A ★★ ★★ · 00:00
00:41 / 16:19		
S 14	02:15 / 10:15 / 18:15 / 22:30	★★ ★ · ♊ 22:00
01:12 / 17:19	WANING	
S 15	02:45 / 11:00 / 19:15 / 23:30	★ ★
01:50 / 18:14	02:18	
M 16	03:30 / 11:45 / 20:00	★ · 00:00
02:36 / 19:02		
T 17	00:15 / 04:30 / 12:45 / 20:45	★
03:29 / 19:43		
W 18	01:00 / 05:30 / 13:30 / 21:15	
04:31 / 20:18	05:25	
T 19	02:00 / 06:30 / 14:15 / 21:45	● · 06:00
05:37 / 20:48		
F 20	02:45 / 07:45 / 15:00 / 22:15	★ · 21:00
06:47 / 21:14		
S 21	03:30 / 09:00 / 16:00 / 22:30	★ ★ ★
08:00 / 21:37	WAXING	
S 22	04:15 / 10:15 / 16:45 / 23:00	★ ★ ★ ★
09:14 / 21:58		
M 23	05:00 / 11:30 / 17:30 / 23:15	★ · 12:00 ★
10:29 / 22:20		

W.2

W.3

JULY

T 24	06:00		
	12:45		
	18:15	★	
11:45 22:43	23:45		♉♂ 23:00

WAXING

W 25	06:45	★	
	14:00		
	19:15		
13:02 23:10			

T 26	00:15 07:45		
	15:15		
	20:00	19:00	
14:21 23:41			

09:57 ◑

F 27	00:45 08:30	★	
	16:45	★	
15:38	21:00	02:00	

S 28	01:15 09:30	☊ 12:00	
	17:45		
00:21 16:50	22:00		

S 29	02:15 10:30	P 10:00	
	19:00		
01:10 17:54	23:00		——— W.31 ———

13:15

M 30	03:15 11:30	05:00 ★	
	19:45	★	
02:11 18:47	00:00	★	

WAXING

T 31	04:15 12:30	★★ ★	
	20:30	★★	
03:21 19:29			

AUGUST

W 1	01:00 05:30	★ 08:00	
	13:30	★	
04:37 20:02	21:00	★	

04:29 ○

T 2	02:00 07:00	★	
	14:15	★	
05:55 20:30	21:30	★	

F 3	02:45 08:15	08:00	
	15:15		
07:12 20:53	22:00	★	

WANING

S 4	03:30 09:30	★	
	16:00		
08:26 21:14	22:15		

S 5	04:15 10:45	06:00 ★★	
	16:45	★	
09:38 21:35	22:30	★	

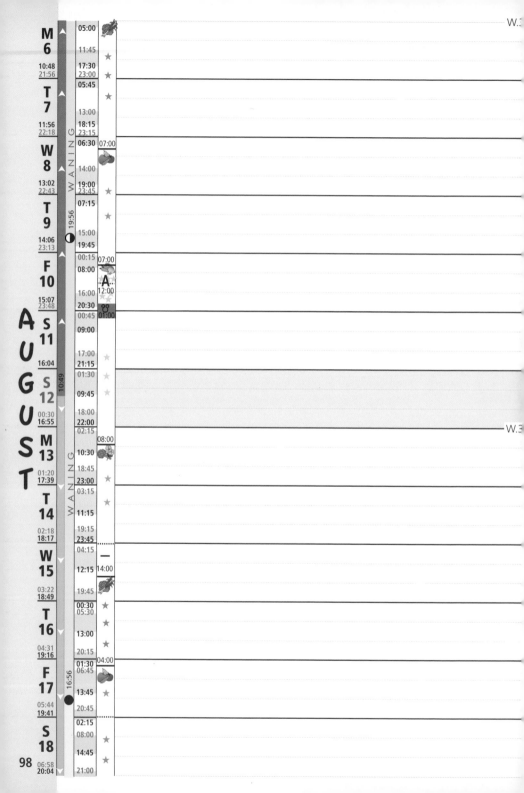

A U G U S T

M 6 10:48 21:56	05:00 11:45 17:30 23:00	★ ★
T 7 11:56 22:18	05:45 13:00 18:15 23:15	★
W 8 13:02 22:43	06:30 07:00 14:00 19:00 23:45	★
T 9 14:06 23:13	07:15 15:00 19:45	★
F 10 15:07 23:48	00:15 07:00 08:00 A 12:00 16:00 20:30 01:00	
S 11 16:04	00:45 09:00 17:00 21:15	★
S 12 00:30 16:55	01:30 09:45 18:00 22:00	★ ★
M 13 01:20 17:39	02:15 08:00 10:30 18:45 23:00	★
T 14 02:18 18:17	03:15 11:15 19:15 23:45	★
W 15 03:22 18:49	04:15 12:15 14:00 19:45	—
T 16 04:31 19:16	00:30 05:30 13:00 20:15	★ ★ ★
F 17 05:44 19:41	01:30 06:45 04:00 13:45 20:45	★
S 18 06:58 20:04	02:15 08:00 14:45 21:00	★ ★

WANING

19:56 10:49 16:56

AUGUST

Day	Sun times	Tide/Moon times	Notes
S 19	08:14 / 20:26	03:00 09:15 15:30 21:30 — 18:00	W.34
M 20	09:32 / 20:50	03:45 10:30 16:15 21:45	☊ ☿ 13:00
T 21	10:50 / 21:15	04:45 11:45 17:15 22:15	
W 22	12:09 / 21:46	05:30 13:15 18:00 22:45 — 01:00	WAXING
T 23	13:27 / 22:22	06:30 14:30 19:00 23:15 — 20:00	P
F 24	14:40 / 23:08	07:30 15:45 20:00 — 07:00 / 13:00	☊ · 14:55
S 25	15:45	00:15 08:30 16:45 21:00	19:45
S 26	00:04 / 16:41	01:00 09:30 17:45 22:00 — 12:00	W.35
M 27	01:09 / 17:26	02:15 10:15 18:30 22:45	WAXING
T 28	02:21 / 18:01	03:15 11:15 19:00 23:45 — 16:00	
W 29	03:36 / 18:31	04:30 12:15 19:30	
T 30	04:52 / 18:56	00:30 05:45 13:00 20:00 — 17:00	
F 31	06:06 / 19:18	01:30 07:00 13:45 20:15	14:59

99

SEPTEMBER

Day	Sun times	Times	
S 1	07:19 19:39	02:15 08:15 14:30 20:45	★★ 14:00
S 2	08:29 20:00	03:00 09:30 15:15 21:00	★ ★
M 3	09:38 20:22	03:45 10:45 16:00 21:15	★
T 4	10:46 20:46	04:30 11:45 16:45 21:45	★ 16:00 ★★
W 5	11:51 21:14	05:15 12:45 17:30 22:15	★ ★ ★
T 6	12:54 21:47	06:00 14:00 18:15 22:45	★ ★ 15:00
F 7	13:52 22:26	06:45 14:45 19:15 23:30	8 03:00 A 07:00 ★ ★
S 8	14:45 23:12	07:30 15:45 20:00	★ ★
S 9	15:32	00:15 08:30 16:30 20:45	★ ★ ★ 16:00
M 10	00:06 16:12	01:00 09:15 17:15 21:30	★ ★
T 11	01:07 16:46	02:00 10:00 17:45 22:30	★ ★ ★ ★ 23:00
W 12	02:13 17:15	03:15 10:45 18:15 23:15	★ ★ ★
T 13	03:23 17:42	04:30 11:45 18:45	13:00 ★ ★

WANING

14:16

19:14

W.3(

W.3

F **14**	0:00 5:30	
04:37 18:06	12:30 19:00	★
S **15**	1:00 7:00	★
05:53 18:29	13:15 19:30	02:00
S **16**	1:45 8:15	
07:11 18:52	14:15 19:45	★

W.38

M **17**	2:30 9:30	
08:31 19:18	15:00 20:15	★ ★
T **18**	3:30 10:45	
09:52 19:48	16:00 20:45	**P** 04:00 07:00
W **19**	4:30 12:15	
11:12 20:23	16:45 21:30	
T **20**	5:15 13:30	13:00 ♌ 14:00
12:29 21:07	17:45 22:00	
F **21**	6:15 14:45	
13:38 22:00	18:45 23:00	★ ★
S **22**	7:15 15:30	
14:36 23:03	19:45	17:00
S **23**	0:00 8:15	
15:24	16:30 20:45	★ ★

W.39

M **24**	1:15 9:15	★
00:12 16:02	17:00 21:45	21:00
T **25**	2:30 10:00	
01:25 16:33	17:30 22:30	★ ★
W **26**	3:45 11:00	
02:39 16:59	18:00 23:15	

WAXING 03:12 01:09 20:42

OCTOBER

W **10**	02:00	
	09:30	★
	16:45	★
01:04 **15:41**	22:00	23:00 ★
T **11**	03:15	
	10:15	
	17:00	
02:14 **16:05**	22:45	★
F **12**	04:30	★
	11:00	
	17:30	
03:28 **16:29**	23:30	
S **13**	05:45	
	12:00	12:00
	17:45	
04:44 **16:52**	00:15	★
S **14**	07:00	★
	12:45	
06:03 **17:17**	18:15	★
M **15** ●	01:15	W.42
	08:30	
	13:45	
07:25 **17:46**	18:45	
T **16**	02:15	
	09:45	
	14:45	16:00
08:48 **18:19**	19:15	★★★
W **17**	03:15	02:00 P
	11:15	
	15:45	19:00
10:09 **19:01**	20:00	21:00
T **18**	04:15	
	12:30	
	16:45	
11:24 **19:52**	20:45	
F **19**	05:15	★
	13:30	
	17:45	
12:28 **20:54**	22:00	00:00
S **20**	06:15	
	14:15	★
	18:45	★
13:21 **22:03**	23:00	
S **21**	07:15	★
	15:00	
	19:30	W.43
14:03 **23:16**	00:15	03:00
M **22** ◑	08:00	—
	15:30	
14:36	20:30	

WANING
WAXING
13:04
07:43
04:33

103

OCTOBER

T 23
00:30
15:03
01:30
09:00 ★
16:00 ★
21:15

W 24
01:43
15:27
02:45 05:00
09:45
16:30
22:00 ★

T 25
02:55
15:48
04:00 ★
10:30
16:45 ★
22:45 ★

F 26
04:04
16:09
05:00 04:00
11:15
17:15
23:30

WAXING

S 27
05:13
16:30
06:15 ★
12:00
17:30 ★

S 28
05:20
15:53
00:15
06:15
11:45
17:00

────────────────────── W.4

M 29
19:51
06:26
16:18
00:00 05:00
07:30
12:30
17:15 ★

T 30
07:30
16:48
00:45
08:30 ★
13:15
17:45

W 31
08:32
17:23
01:30
09:30
14:00 11:00
18:30

NOVEMBER

T 1
09:28
18:04
08:17
02:30
10:30 ★★
14:45 A
19:00 15:00
        ★

F 2
10:19
18:51
03:15
11:15 ★
15:30
19:45 ★

WANING

S 3
11:04
19:46
04:00 06:00
12:00
16:30
20:45

S 4
11:41
20:45
04:45 ★
12:45
17:15
21:45 ★

────────────────────── W.4

M 5
104 12:14
21:49
05:30
13:15 14:00
18:00
22:45 ★

NOVEMBER

Day	Times		
T 6 12:41 / 22:57	06:15	13:45	18:45
00:37			
W 7 13:06	00:00 / 06:00 07:15	14:00	19:30
T 8 00:07 / 13:29	01:00 08:00	14:30	20:15
F 9 01:19 / 13:52	02:15 08:45	14:45	21:00 / 22:00
S 10 02:35 / 14:15	03:30 09:30	15:15	22:00
S 11 03:53 / 14:41	05:00 10:30	15:45	22:45
M 12 05:15 / 15:12	06:15 11:15	16:15	23:45
T 13 06:38 / 15:50	07:45 12:15	16:45	02:00
22:09			
W 14 07:58 / 16:37	00:45 09:00	13:15	17:30 — 05:00 / 07:00 — P 10:00
T 15 09:10 / 17:36	01:45 10:15	14:30	18:30
16:04			
F 16 10:11 / 18:45	03:00 11:15	15:30	19:45 — 08:00
S 17 10:59 / 20:00	04:00 12:00	16:30	21:00
S 18 11:36 / 21:16	05:00 12:30	17:15	22:15 — 09:00
M 19 12:07 / 22:32	05:45 13:00	18:15	23:30

WANING

WAXING

W.46

W.47

NOVEMBER

T **20**	14:33 ◐	06:45
		10:00
12:32 23:45		13:30
		19:00 ★
W **21**		00:45
		07:30 ★
		14:00 ★
12:54		19:45 ★
T **22**		02:00
		08:15 09:00
		14:15
00:56 13:15		20:30
F **23**		03:00
		09:00
		14:30 ★
02:04 13:36		21:15
S **24**	WAXING	04:15 ★
		09:45
		15:00
03:11 13:58		22:00
S **25**		05:15
		10:30 11:00
		15:15
04:17 14:22		22:45

W.48

M **26**		06:15 ★
		11:15 ★
		15:45 ★
05:22 14:50		23:30
T **27**		07:30 ★
		12:00 11:00
		16:30 ♉ 17:00
06:24 15:23		
W **28**	14:47 ○	00:15
		08:15 ★
		12:45 A
07:22 16:01		17:00 20:00
T **29**	14:32	01:00
		09:15 ★
		13:30 ★
08:16 16:47		17:45 ★
F **30**		02:00
		10:00 12:00
		14:15
09:02 17:39		18:45

DECEMBER

S **1**	WANING	02:45
		10:45
		15:15 ★
09:42 18:37		19:30 ★
S **2**		03:30
		11:15
		16:00 20:00
10:16 19:40		20:45

W.49

M **3**		04:15
		11:45 ★ ★
		16:45 ★
106 10:45 20:45		21:45 —

DECEMBER

Day		Times
T 4	11:10 / 21:53	05:00 · 12:15 · 13:00 · 17:30 · 23:00
W 5	11:33 / 23:03	05:45 · 12:30 · 18:15
T 6	11:55	00:00 · 06:30 · 13:00 · 19:00
F 7	00:14 / 12:17	01:15 · 06:00 · 07:15 · 13:15 · 19:45
S 8	01:29 / 12:41	02:30 · 08:15 · 13:45 · 20:30
S 9	02:46 / 13:08	03:45 · 09:00 · 14:15 · 21:30
M 10	04:06 / 13:41	05:00 · 10:00 · 13:00 · 14:45 · 22:30
T 11	05:26 / 14:22	06:30 · 11:00 · 15:15 · 16:00 · 18:00 · 23:30
W 12	06:43 / 15:14	07:45 · 12:00 · 16:15 · 23:00
T 13	07:51 / 16:18	00:30 · P · 08:45 · 13:00 · 17:15 · 19:00
F 14	08:47 / 17:32	01:30 · 09:45 · 14:00 · 18:30
S 15	09:31 / 18:51	02:45 · 10:30 · 15:00 · 19:00 · 19:45
S 16	10:06 / 20:10	03:30 · 11:00 · 16:00 · 21:15
M 17	10:34 / 21:27	04:30 · 11:30 · 17:00 · 22:30

15:33

WANING

W.50

03:42 · 08:43

WAXING

W.51

107

D E C E M B E R

T 18
10:58
22:41

05:15
12:00 ★
17:45
23:45 ★

W 19
11:20
23:52

05:20

06:00
12:15
18:30
15:00

T 20
11:42

00:45
07:00
12:45
19:15 ★

F 21
01:01
12:03

02:00
07:30 ★
13:00
20:00

S 22
02:08
12:27

03:15
08:15
13:30
20:45
17:00

S 23
03:13
12:53

WAXING

04:15
09:00
14:00 ★
21:30

M 24
04:16
13:24

05:15
10:00
14:30
22:15
17:00
22:00
☿ ♀ 18:00

T 25
05:16
14:00

06:15
10:45 ★
15:00 ★
23:00
21:00
A

W 26
06:11
14:44

21:25

07:15 ★
11:30
15:45 ★
23:45

T 27
07:00
15:34

10:22

08:00
12:15
16:30
18:00

F 28
07:43
16:30

○

00:45 ★
08:45 ★ ★
13:00
17:30
....

S 29
08:19
17:32

01:30 ★
09:15 ★
13:45
18:30

S 30
08:50
18:37

WANING

02:00
02:15
09:45 ★
14:45
19:30 ★

M 31
09:16
19:44

03:00 ★
10:15
15:30
20:45
19:00

08

W.52

W.53

Plan of your garden

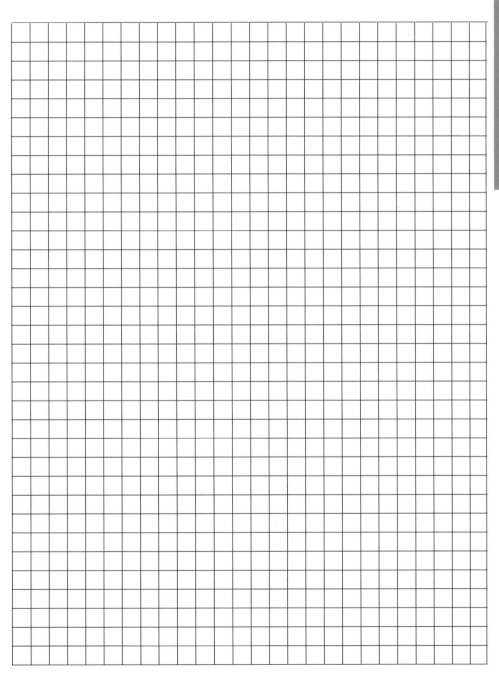

Companion planting

Plants release secretions into the soil via their roots so one plant can affect the growth of another nearby. The Chinese and the South American Indians have known about this and made good use of the knowledge for centuries. Organizing your garden so that you position those plants that have a beneficial effect on each other side by side is another way to help improve your gardening success. Try your own companion planting experiments; results will vary according to the type of soil.

Plant	Grows well with	Does not grow well with
Asparagus	Cucumber, leek, parsley, pea, tomato	Beetroot, garlic, onion
Aubergine	French bean	Potato
Beetroot	Cabbage, celery, lettuce, onion	Asparagus, carrot, leek, runner bean, tomato
Cabbage (except kohlrabi)	Beetroot, celery, corn salad, French bean, lettuce, onion, pea, potato, tomato	Chicory, fennel, garlic, leek, parsnip, radish
Carrot	Chervil, chive, dwarf French bean, lettuce, onion, leek, parsley, parsnip, pea, radish, tomato	Beetroot, Swiss chard
Celery	Beetroot, cabbage, cucurbitaceous plants, French bean, leek, pea, Swiss chard, tomato	Lettuce, maize, parsley
Chicory		Cabbage
Corn salad	Cabbage, leek, onion, strawberry	
Cucumber	Asparagus, basil, cabbage, celery, chive, French bean, lettuce, maize, pea	Potato, radish, tomato
Fennel	Celery, leek tomato	Cabbage, French bean, parsnip,
French bean	Aubergine, carrot, celery, cabbage, lettuce, maize, marigold, potato, spinach, radish, strawberry, turnip	Beetroot, garlic, fennel, onion, shallot, Swiss chard
Garlic	Potato, strawberry	Cabbage, French bean, marigold, pea

Plant	Grows well with	Does not grow well with
Kohlrabi	Beetroot, celery, leek, lettuce	Chicory, fennel, radish, strawberry
Leek	Asparagus, carrot, celery, fennel, lettuce, onion, strawberry, tomato	Beetroot, cabbage, parsley, pea, Swiss chard
Lettuce	Beetroot, cabbage, carrot, chervil, cucumber, broad bean, leek, onion, pea, strawberry, radish, turnip	Parsley
Maize	Cucurbitaceous plants, French beans, pea, potato, tomato	Beetroot, celery
Marrow and courgette	Basil, maize, nasturtium	Potato, radish
Onion	Beetroot, carrot, cucumber, leek, lettuce, parsley, parsnip, strawberry, tomato	Cabbage, French bean, pea, potato
Parsnip	Carrot, onion	Fennel
Pea	Asparagus, cabbage, carrot, celery, cucumber, lettuce, maize, potato, radish, turnip	Garlic, leek, onion, parsley, shallot
Potato	Broad bean, cabbage, celery, French bean, garlic, marigold, nasturtium, pea, tomato	Aubergine, cucumber, maize, onion
Radish	Carrot, chervil, French bean, garlic, lettuce, pea, spinach, tomato	Cabbage, marrow
Spinach	Cabbage, French bean, radish, strawberry, turnip	Beetroot, Swiss chard
Strawberry	Chive, corn salad, French bean, garlic, leek, lettuce, marigold, onion, spinach, thyme, turnip	Cabbage
Swiss chard	Celery, lettuce, onion	Asparagus, basil, leek, tomato
Tomato	Asparagus, basil, carrot, garlic, cabbage, celery, leek, French marigold, nasturtium, marigold, onion, parsley, parsnip, potato, radish	Beetroot, fennel, kohlrabi, pea, Swiss chard
Turnip	French bean, lettuce, pea, spinach	

Index